£1.50

Happy [illegible] ...d

& don't miss page 50!

Graham, Barbara & Esther xxx

27. 10. 2007

NOTTS COUNTY
A Pictorial History

The highs and lows of the world's oldest professional football club

By Paul Wain
with additional material from Colin Slater

Published by
Yore Publications
12 The Furrows,
Harefield,
Middx. UB9 6AT

British Library Cataloguing-in-Publication Data.
A catalogue record for this book
is available from the British Library.

ISBN 0954783034

Printed and bound by
Cromwell Press Ltd.
Trowbridge

Introduction by Paul Wain

More than 125 different clubs have played in the Football League at some time since 1888. In common with about 100 of them, Notts County's history does not involve much by way of major trophies and glittering achievements but there is still a colourful story to be told.

Supporters have fond memories of favourite players, special matches, great goals, promotion seasons, cup runs, giant-killing and tussles with local rivals. Legends grow as older generations pass on tales of the past. Notts County are also in the unique position of being the oldest of all the world's professional clubs, as well as being one of the 12 founder members of the League. They have played in every division.

I started supporting Notts at the age of seven because they were my father's team and his father's before that. I remember when my grandfather gave me my first copy of the *Post Football Guide*. In it I saw that the club had been promoted several times as champions of their division. They had played for many seasons in the First Division and they had even won the FA Cup. I also read that Notts had had a number of international players - Greenhalgh, Cursham, Macrae, Dobson, Moore and others - going as far back as the 1870s.

Years later a new dimension opened when I saw for the first time a photograph of the Notts team that won the Cup. It then became a hobby to search for other photographs and memorabilia, especially programmes, which brought to life the names and facts in the football annuals. In this book I am very pleased to share some of the highlights of that search with others who are interested in the history of Notts County or in football history generally. All the club's promotions, best cup runs, most notable players, Wembley visits and other major events, from the 1860s onwards, are featured in the illustrations.

In normal times the tendency would be to focus only on the highs. However, these are not normal times and a low point has been hit. A financial crisis within the last three years brought the club very close to extinction and events off the pitch have been mirrored by poor results on it. A similar situation existed in the mid-1960s and a less severe one in the mid-1980s. The only person who knows the inside story of all these events is Colin Slater, the Nottingham writer and broadcaster. He has reported from the Meadow Lane press box since1959 and has been known as *"The Voice of Notts County"* since BBC Radio Nottingham went on air in 1968. Although this book is primarily a pictorial history, Colin's personal recollections of the crises have been added because we simply cannot ignore the club's fight for survival or the efforts of the many people, supporters and others, who have worked so hard to keep Notts going.

Let's hope the Magpies will duly celebrate their 150th anniversary in 2012 and that the publications of the day will report that the gloom of 2004 soon lifted.

Paul Wain October 2004

Acknowledgements

This book has been made possible thanks to the help of all those listed below who, whether recently or years ago, very kindly made available photographs, scrapbooks, memorabilia or other information concerning Notts County:

The Nottingham Evening Post and their Deputy Librarian, Phil Meakin (a Forest supporter!).

Keith Warsop. It is thanks to many years of extensive research by Keith that there exists a detailed knowledge of the club's history from the earliest times. His own book, 'The Magpies', was published in 1984 by Sporting And Leisure Press but is now long out of print.

Colin Slater

The staff at Notts County: Mark Stevenson, Mark Durkin, Charlotte Moore.

Former players: 'Paddy' Mills, Harold Andrews, Alf Feebery, Jackie Sewell, Billy Baxter, Harry Adamson, Aubrey Southwell, Tommy Deans, Roy Kirkham, Pat Groome, Les Bradd.

The relatives of the following former players: Fred Rothera, Harry Cursham, Albert Iremonger, Bert Morley, Arthur Clamp, Albert Waterall, Billy Death, Percy Mills, Bill Corkhill, Alex Gibson.

Plus: Claude Bishop, Bill Hopcroft, John Mounteney, Jack Wheeler, Peter Thompson. Peter Wynne-Thomas (librarian of Nottinghamshire County Cricket Club), Miss C. L. Betts, Brian Tansley, Tony Brown, Dave Twydell, Gareth Davies., Max Hopkinson

Every effort has been made to trace the source of illustrations and to ensure that copyright has not been infringed. I offer my apologies to anyone whose name I have inadvertently omitted.

Paul Wain

TO

THE

FUTURE

THE NOTTS COUNTY PICTORIAL HISTORY

CONTENTS

1: Pre-League Years: 1862-1888

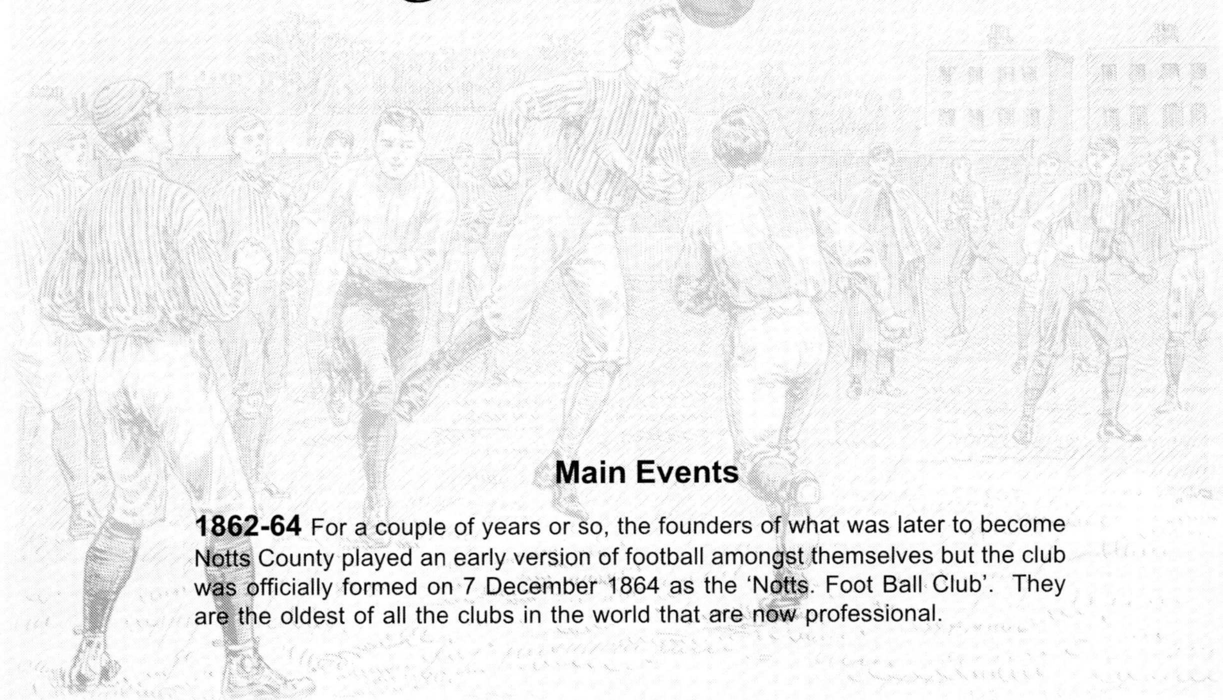

Main Events

1862-64 For a couple of years or so, the founders of what was later to become Notts County played an early version of football amongst themselves but the club was officially formed on 7 December 1864 as the 'Notts. Foot Ball Club'. They are the oldest of all the clubs in the world that are now professional.

1864-88 Friendly matches were arranged with other clubs in England and Scotland. In the first half of the 1880s Notts were one of the best clubs in the country, at their peak fielding up to 8 England internationals in the same team. They first entered the FA Cup in 1877/8 and had several good runs, reaching the semi-finals in 1883 and again in1884. In 1885 and 1887 they reached the round before the semi-finals.

Notable Players

Over 50 goals – Harry Cursham (initials H.A.), Arthur Cursham (A.W.), Harry Jackson, William Gunn.
Over 80 appearances – Ernest Greenhalgh (E.H.), Albert Moore (A.E.), H. Chapman, Harry Daft, Harry Cursham, Arthur Cursham, Harry Jackson, Charley Dobson (C.F.), Alf Dobson (A.T.C.), Harry Moore (H.T.), Herbert Emmitt, William Gunn.
Internationals – Ernest Greenhalgh, Harry Cursham, Arthur Cursham, John Dixon, Alfred Dobson, Charley Dobson, William Gunn, Stuart Macrae, Harry Moore and Harold Morse (all played for England). John Morgan (J.R.) played for Wales.

Three who played for Notts in the 1860s

1: Ernest Greenhalgh was one of the first Notts 'stars'. He played in defence in 147 games between 1869 -1883 and was captain from 1872 onwards. He was the club's first international, appearing twice for England in 1872/3 and was one of four brothers who played for Notts.

2: Richard Daft was one of the pioneers of the club and played in1864/5 in the first-ever match for which the line-up is known. He played several times until early 1871/2 and was also a successful cricketer for Nottinghamshire.

3: Fred Rothera (initials F.W.) played in 48 games between 1869 and 1877. This photograph was taken in the 1890s

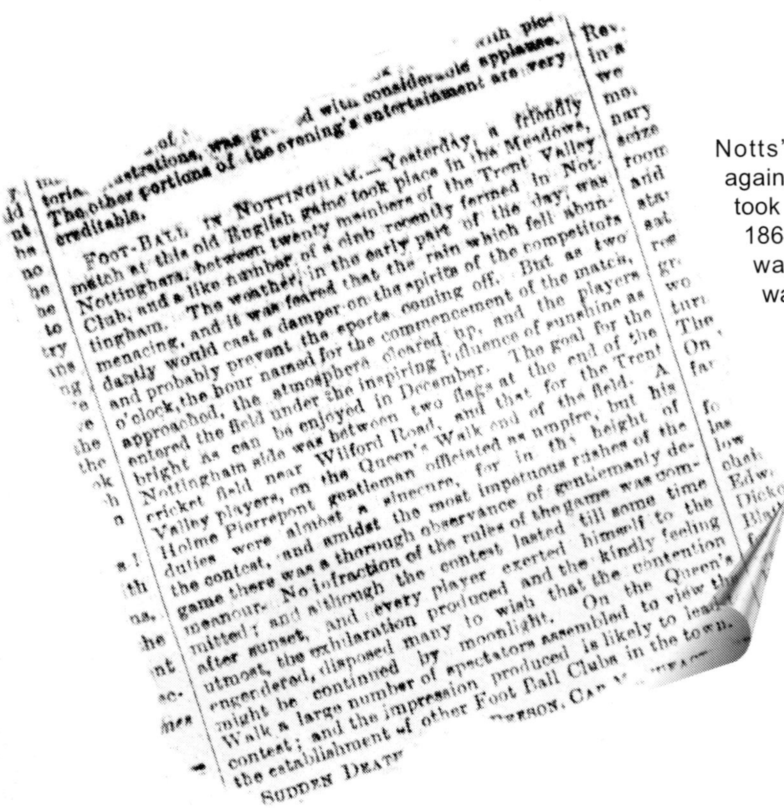

... with pictorial illustrations, was gr... with considerable applause. The other portions of the evening's entertainment are very creditable.

FOOT-BALL IN NOTTINGHAM.—Yesterday, a friendly match at this old English game took place in the Meadows, Nottingham, between twenty members of the Trent Valley Club, and a like number of a club recently formed in Nottingham. The weather, in the early part of the day, was menacing, and it was feared that the rain which fell abundantly would cast a damper on the spirits of the competitors and probably prevent the sports coming off. But as two o'clock, the hour named for the commencement of the match, approached, the atmosphere cleared up, and the players entered the field under the inspiring influence of sunshine as bright as can be enjoyed in December. The goal for the Nottingham side was between two flags at the end of the cricket field near Wilford Road, and that for the Trent Valley players, on the Queen's Walk end of the field. A Holme Pierrepont gentleman officiated as umpire, but his duties were almost a sinecure, for in the height of the contest, and amidst the most impetuous rushes of the game there was a thorough observance of gentlemanly demeanour. No infraction of the rules of the game was committed; and although the contest lasted till some time after sunset, and every player exerted himself to the utmost, the exhilaration produced and the kindly feeling engendered, disposed many to wish that the contention might be continued by moonlight. On the Queen's Walk a large number of spectators assembled to view the contest; and the impression produced is likely to lead to the establishment of other Foot Ball Clubs in the town.

SUDDEN DEATH ... [illegible]ERSON. CAR...

Notts' first-ever match against external opponents took place on 8 December 1864, the day after the club was officially formed. It was against Trent Valley.

This is the oldest photograph of Notts County known to have survived. They played at the time in amber and black hoops. It is the team that faced a London representative side at Trent Bridge cricket ground on 17 March 1873 (left to right): **Standing:** F. Marriott, W. Mason, W.H. Revis. **Sitting:** J. Parr, S.W. Widdowson, A. Bright, W.M. Robinson **Front:** A.W. (Arthur) Cursham, G.Hayes, E.H. (Ernest) Greenhalgh, C.J. Spencer.

Friendly games in pre-League days

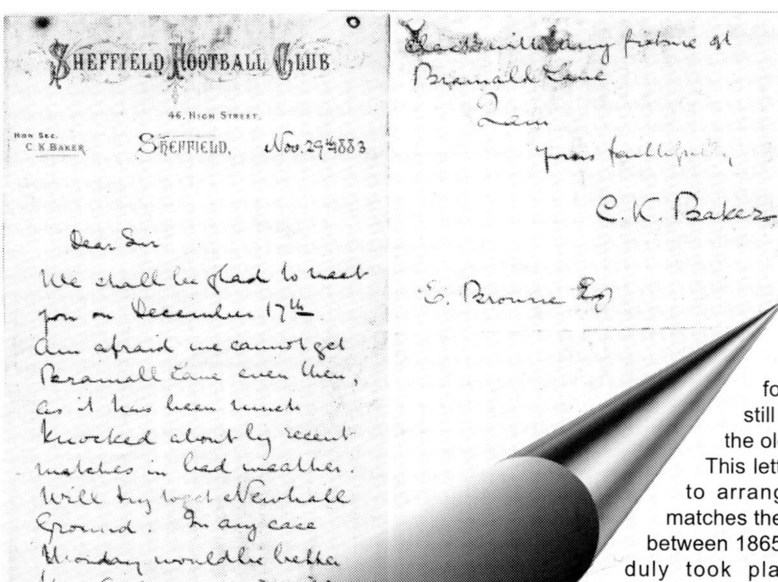

SHEFFIELD FOOTBALL CLUB

46, HIGH STREET,

HON SEC.
C. K BAKER

SHEFFIELD, Nov. 29th 1883

Dear Sir

We shall be glad to meet you on December 17th. Am afraid we cannot get Bramall Lane even then, as it has been much knocked about by recent matches in bad weather. Will try to get Newhall Ground. In any case Monday would be better than Saturday as it will not [illegible] fixture at Bramall Lane [illegible]

Yours faithfully,

C. K. Baker

E. Browne Esq

Sheffield, the amateur club, was founded in 1857 and is still in existence, making it the oldest football club of all. This letter was written in 1883 to arrange one of almost 50 matches they played against Notts between 1865 and 1887. The game duly took place on Monday, 17 December 1883 and was a 1-1 draw.

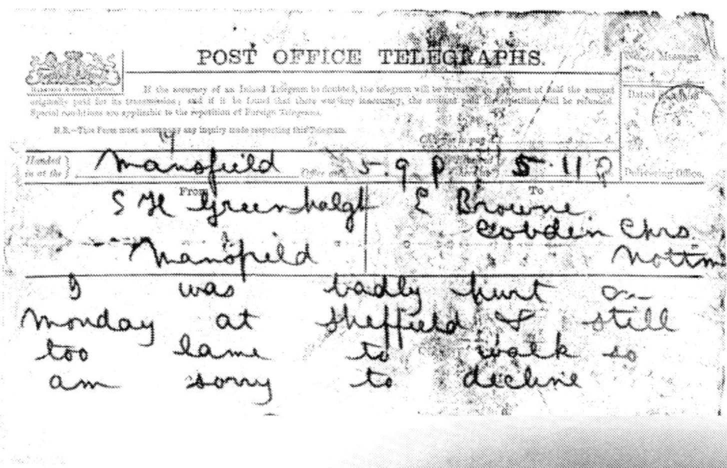
POST OFFICE TELEGRAPHS.

Mansfield 5.9 P 5.11 P

From S H Greenhalgh Mansfield

To E Browne Cobden Chas Nottm

I was badly hurt on monday at Sheffield & still too lame to walk so am sorry to decline

In this telegram to the Notts secretary dated 19 December 1883, Ernest Greenhalgh refers to a bad injury received in the game at Sheffield two days earlier. It was the last time he ever played for Notts.

The oldest Scottish club, amateurs Queens Park, were founded in 1867 and were a major force in early football. They played Notts 20 times between 1875 and 1888. This is the Notts team that played them in Glasgow on 17 November 1877 (it was also Fred Rothera's last game). They are wearing white shirts to avoid a clash with Queens Park's hoops: **Standing:** Erasmus Keely, Fred Rothera, Arthur Ashwell (umpire), Harold Greenhalgh, Harry Cursham, George Seals. **Sitting:** Richard Greenhalgh, Arthur Cursham, Ernest Greenhalgh, Tom Oliver, S.H. Keely. **Front:** Henry Jessop.

(Right) J.R. (John) Morgan played only 3 games for Notts in 1879/80 but in that period played twice for Wales, making him the club's first Welsh international.

Some of the great players of the 1870s and 1880s

(Below) **Stuart Macrae**, a half-back, played more than 75 games from 1879 to 1887. He was born in Scotland but appeared 6 times for England.

Arthur Cursham played over 140 games and scored more than 60 goals between 1871 and 1884. He played for and captained England. He also played cricket for Nottinghamshire and Derbyshire. After his last game for Notts in April 1884, he emigrated to Florida to run an orange plantation and tragically died there with malaria on Xmas Eve the same year. He was 31.

Harry Cursham, brother of Arthur, was the most prolific goalscorer of the era with at least 208 goals in 227 appearances or more between 1877 and 1891. 49 of those goals came in FA Cup games, which is still the national record for the competition (Ian Rush comes next with 44). He played 8 times for England and is pictured here in the England strip.

(Above) **John Dixon**, inside-left, played over 60 matches from 1883 to 1888, when he retired owing to ill-health. He made one appearance for England. He is pictured playing cricket for Nottinghamshire, who he served with distinction for many years.

(Above) William or **Billy Gunn**, a 6' 2" winger, played more than 140 games and scored over 60 goals between 1882 and 1893. He also became a director of the club before he finished playing. He was an outstanding cricketer for Nottinghamshire and played for England at both cricket and football.

The FA Cup runs of the 1880s

The side that played in the FA Cup semi-final against Blackburn Rovers on 1 March 1884 included 8 England internationals. The club colours had been changed to chocolate and Cambridge blue halves in December 1880.(Left to right): **Standing:** Arthur Ashwell (umpire), John Dixon, Herbert Emmitt, William Gunn, Harry Moore, Alf Dobson.. **Sitting:** Mordecai Sherwin, Arthur Cursham, Stuart Macrae. **Front:** Charley Dobson, Harry Cursham, H. Chapman.

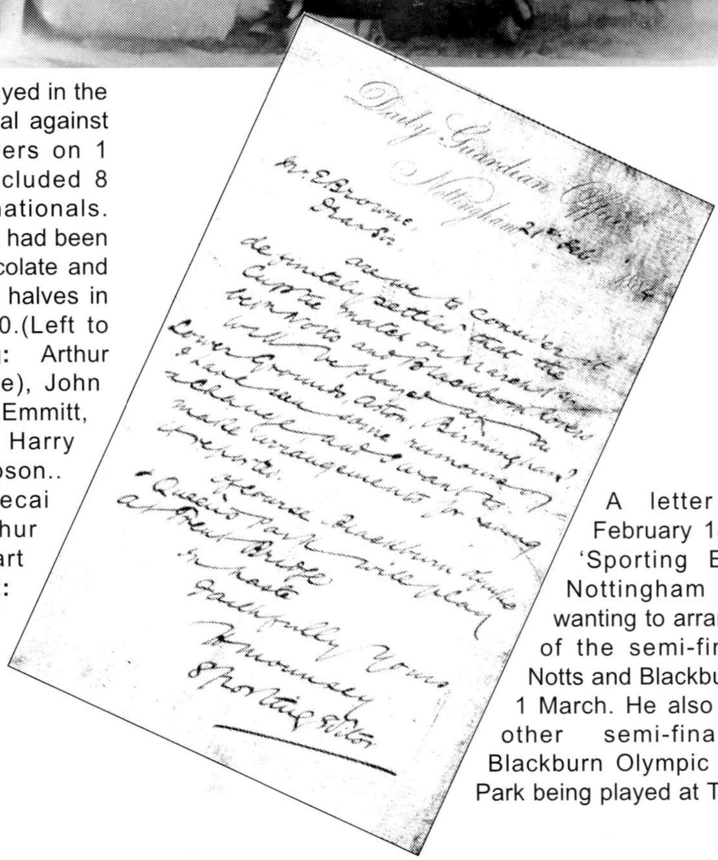

Daily Guardian Office
Nottingham 21st Feb 1884

Mr E. Browne,
Dear Sir,

Faithfully Yours
Sporting Editor

A letter dated 21 February 1884 from the 'Sporting Editor' of a Nottingham newspaper wanting to arrange coverage of the semi-final between Notts and Blackburn Rovers on 1 March. He also refers to the other semi-final between Blackburn Olympic and Queens Park being played at Trent Bridge.

(Left) The team that met Queens Park in the FA Cup 6th round and the replay in February 1885. It included 7 England internationals and Harry Cursham later considered it to be the best Notts side he played in (left to right): **Standing:** Stuart Macrae, Charley Dobson, William Gunn, John Dixon. **Sitting:** Harry Cursham, Alf Dobson, Harry Moore , Herbert Emmitt. **Front:** Albert Moore, George Coulby, Harry Jackson.

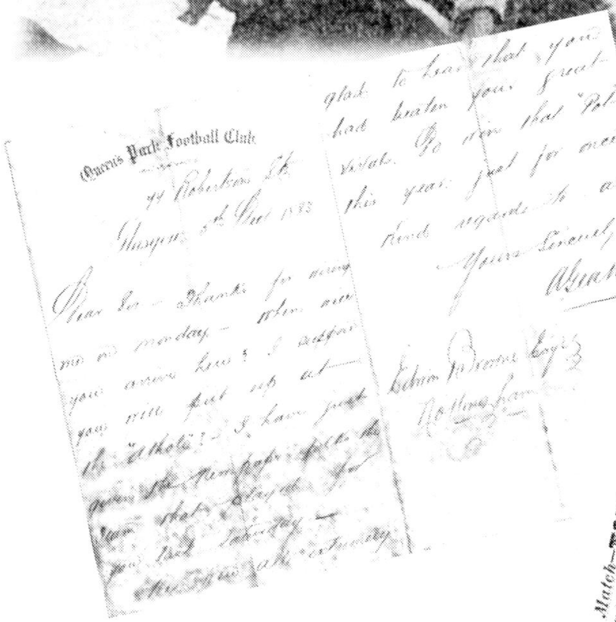

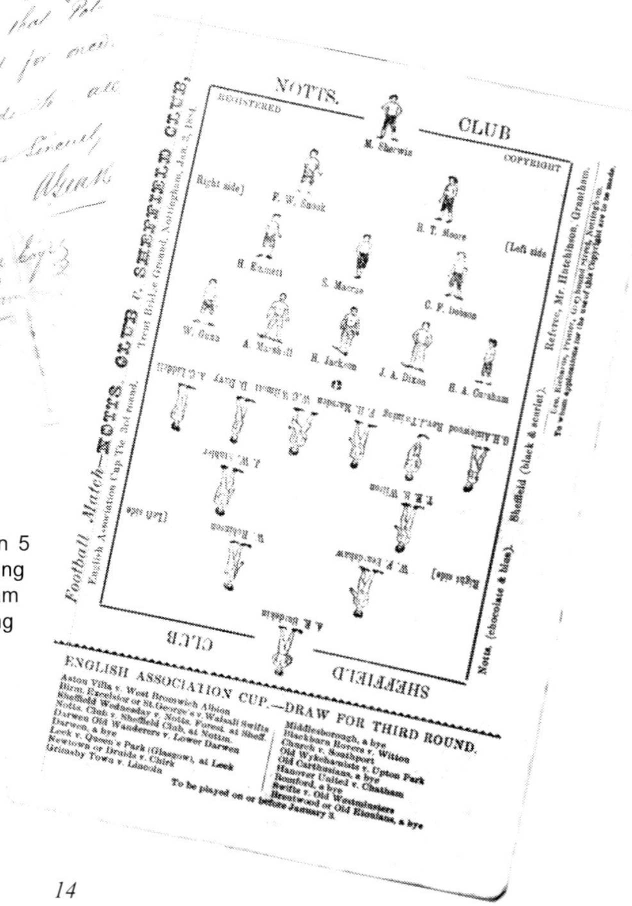

(Above) A letter from Queens Park written on 5 December 1883, congratulating Notts on beating their "great rivals" (they had beaten Nottingham Forest in the FA Cup 4 days earlier) and urging them to "win that 'pot' this year just for once".

(Right) The programme for the 3rd round FA Cup tie between the world's oldest amateur club, Sheffield, and the world's oldest professional club. The match took place on 3 January 1885 (not 1884, which was printed in error).

2: Early League Years: 1888/89 to 1899/00

Main Events

1888/9 Notts were one of the 12 founder members of the Football League.

1890/1 One of the club's best-ever seasons: third in the League and FA Cup Finalists.

1892/3 Relegated to Division 2.

1893/4 FA Cup winners. The first Second Division side to win the Cup.

1896/7 Promoted to Division 1 after 'test matches' (the equivalent of play-offs). Champions of Division 2.

Notable Players

Over 50 goals: Dan Bruce, Harry Daft, James Oswald, Walter Bull

Over 200 appearances: Walter Bull, David Calderhead, Alf Shelton, George Toone

Internationals : Harry Daft, Alf Shelton, George Toone (all played for England)

Others: Jimmy Logan, Tom McInnes, Alex Maconnachie.

S, MONDAY. SEPTEMBER 17,

THE FOOTBALL LEAGUE.

Six League matches took place on Saturday, the attendance at the various games, according to the reporters' estimates, reaching the large number of 26,000 people. Considering that the football season has only just commenced, and that teams are as yet far from being in good playing form, the League promises to be a paying concern for the select band who operated the movement. The results of the matches, with a brief description of the play, are appended :—

EVERTON v. NOTTS. CLUB.

This, the first match of the Notts. Club's League fixtures, was played at Everton on Saturday, before six thousand people. The early play was somewhat in favour of Notts., and Harker was near scoring from a miskick by one of the Everton backs. Then Dick made a long well-judged kick, nicely placing the ball in goal, and Chadwick scored from the partial return of Holland. The Everton forwards showed improved play, and the game was in their favour, though Hodder made several good spins on the left and forced Ross to concede corners. When half-time arrived Everton were leading by one goal to none. On resuming Smalley early on had a difficult shot to stop, and then from a free kick for a foul Ross kicked a second goal. Play continued exciting, and Fleming was cheered for a good run and fine centre, Lewis kicking over, Moore immediately doing the same at the other end. Even play followed, Ross and M'Kenny nicely stopping combined runs by the Notts. forwards. By good play Notts. won a corner, but "hands" against them staved off danger. After even play Notts. scored a nice goal. Jardine in the centre passed neatly and well for Notts., who showed very promising form. They could not score again, however, and retired beaten after an excellent game by two goals to one.—Teams :—

EVERTON.—Smalley, goal ; Ross and Dick, backs ; Dobson, M'Kennion, and Holt, half-backs ; Farmer, Chadwick, Lewis, Waugh, and Fleming, forwards.

NOTTS.—Holland, goal ; M'Lean and Guttridge, backs ; Warburton, Brown, and A. Shelton, half-backs ; Wardle and Moore, right wing ; Jardine, centre ; Hodder and Harker, left wing. Umpire, C. Shelton.

DERBY COUNTY v. WEST BROMWICH ALBION.—Played at Derby in warm weather and in the pre-

The first League match

Notts' first-ever League match was at Everton on 15 September 1888. They lost 2-1 and the scorer of the first League goal was Albert Moore.

Frank Guttridge played right-back in the first League match and was a regular for what was his only full season with Notts. Others who played in the first match and whose photographs appear elsewhere in this book were Albert Moore, Tom McLean and Alf Shelton.

1890/1 – The side that played in the Cup Final and finished 3rd in the League.

The regular League side was Toone, McLean, Hendry, Osborne, Calderhead, Shelton, McGregor, McInnes, Oswald, Locker and Daft. Toone and McLean were injured at the time of the 1891 FA Cup Final and were replaced by Thraves and Ferguson.

No photograph has been found for 1890/1. The closest is this team group taken on 7 November 1891, which also includes a few new signings for the 1891/ 2 season. The now-familiar black and white stripes had been introduced at the start of 1890/1. **Back:** Harry Kirk (Trainer), Charlie Bramley, David Calderhead, George Toone, Jack Hendry, Alf Shelton. **Front:** Tom McLean, James Burns, Tom McInnes, Jimmy Oswald, Harry Walkerdine, Harry Daft.

(Left)
Jimmy Thraves made only 2 League appearances but played in goal in the Final and most of the other Cup games in place of Toone, who missed the last few weeks of the season with a broken leg.

(Right)
Archie Osborne, right-half.

Andrew McGregor, outside-right.

Billy Locker, inside-left. This photograph was taken in 1903 when he played for a team of Notts veterans in a charity match.

Ferguson in this ... take his place.

ALEXANDER FERGUSON, who will take McLean's place as right full back, is a Glasgow native. He played for several clubs in that city before coming to Nottingham. The last club he was connected with in Scotland was the Glasgow Rangers. Originally a full back, he joined Notts, to play right half-back, and in that position last season he was only moderately successful, his play not coming up to the standard of either Calderhead or Shelton. He was relegated to the Reserve at the commencement ... present season, and ... them has played in

Alex 'Sandy' Ferguson played only twice in the League and his only cup match was the Final, in which he replaced the injured McLean. He died just 3 years later, shortly before Notts won the Cup.

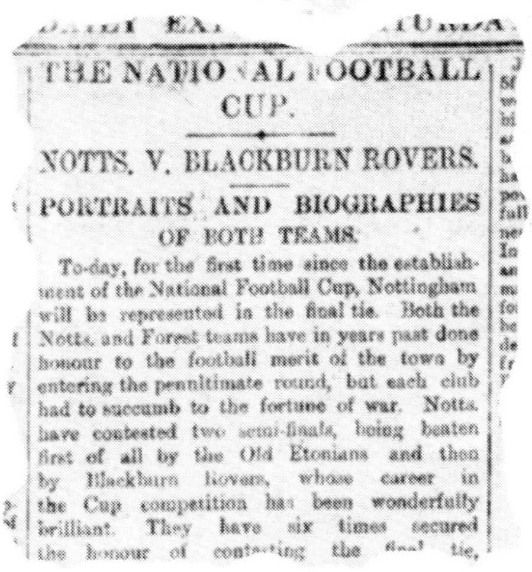

THE NATIO AL OOTBALL CUP.

NOTTS. V. BLACKBURN ROVERS.

PORTRAITS AND BIOGRAPHIES OF BOTH TEAMS.

To-day, for the first time since the establishment of the National Football Cup, Nottingham will be represented in the final tie. Both the Notts. and Forest teams have in years past done honour to the football merit of the town by entering the penultimate round, but each club had to succumb to the fortune of war. Notts. have contested two semi-finals, being beaten first of all by the Old Etonians and then by Blackburn Rovers, whose career in the Cup competition has been wonderfully brilliant. They have six times secured the honour of contesting the final tie,

The Cup Final was on 21 March 1891 at Kennington Oval. Notts lost 3-1 to Blackburn Rovers.

Harry Daft, an outside-left, was the son of the early Notts player Richard. He was the only player to appear in a large number of games both before and after the start of the League, between 1885 and 1894. He played 5 times for England and also played cricket for Nottinghamshire.

1894 FA Cup winners

NOTTS. BRING THE CUP TO NOTTINGHAM

THE VICTORY AT GOODISON PARK

IMPRESSIONS AND COMMENTS

THE GAME DESCRIBED

After twenty years of football the English Cup has come to Nottingham, and "Notts." will be inscribed side by side on its shield with the names of the most famous of other English clubs. For years the great success has been the dream of Notts. enthusiasts, and at length it has come to pass, deservedly indeed, for no organisation has made more generally brilliant and resolute efforts, with a greater share of ill luck. The triumph of Saturday was thoroughly well earned, for at all points Notts. proved the superiors of their opponents. Bolton were indeed out-manœuvred and out-fought. The score of four to one was one of the highest for years in the football final. It came somewhat in the nature of a surprise, for few expected that, whichever side won, more than a single goal would represent the margin. As the ... at P... ...Blackburn Rovers

... Lord Henry Bentinck.

THE HOME-COMING

SCENES IN THE STREETS OF NOTTINGHAM.

Has Nottingham ever turned out into its streets in stronger force, or been more excited, than on Saturday night, when the shabby little English Cup was brought triumphantly to the town for the first time? By nine o'clock there was a very perceptible movement stationwards. By half-past nine Carrington-street had a lining of sight-seers, and the ranks were several deep about the junction with Station-street, while thousands were congregated in front of the station. By ten there was a continuous crowd from St. Peter's Church to the station, while from Canal-street onwards there was only a narrow line left for the passage of cabs, and Station-street was so thronged that a spectator, somewhat deficient in arithmetic, kept exclaiming in tones of triumphant admiration, "I'll bet there's as many people here as there was at Liverpool." Station-street is a miserably gloomy thoroughfare that would smudge out any spectacle, but though it concealed the sights it could not smother the noise—the cheerful effervescence of a huge crowd in a state of intense delight. The only bit of colour in the street was where the Wellington Hotel, by a display of night-lights in rows of claret glasses at the windows of each storey, made the surrounding darkness more dully visible. The darkness and the clatter of the youths' heels on the en... ...ment sheets ... were

(Top) The side that won the FA Cup, beating Bolton Wanderers 4-1 on 31 March 1894 at Goodison Park, Liverpool. Back (l to r): Charlie Bramley, Theophilus Harper, David Calderhead, George Toone, Jack Hendry, Alf Shelton, Joe Goode (trainer). **Front:** Arthur Watson, Sam Donnelly, Jimmy Logan, Dan Bruce, Harry Daft.

(Left) **Jimmy Logan** scored a hat-trick in the Final – one of only 3 players ever to do so (the others were Townsley of Blackburn Rovers in 1890 and Mortensen of Blackpool in 1953). He scored a total of 37 League and Cup goals in 48 games for Notts in seasons 1893/4 and 1894/5. He died in 1896 from pneumonia caught after playing a game for Loughborough Town. He was 25.

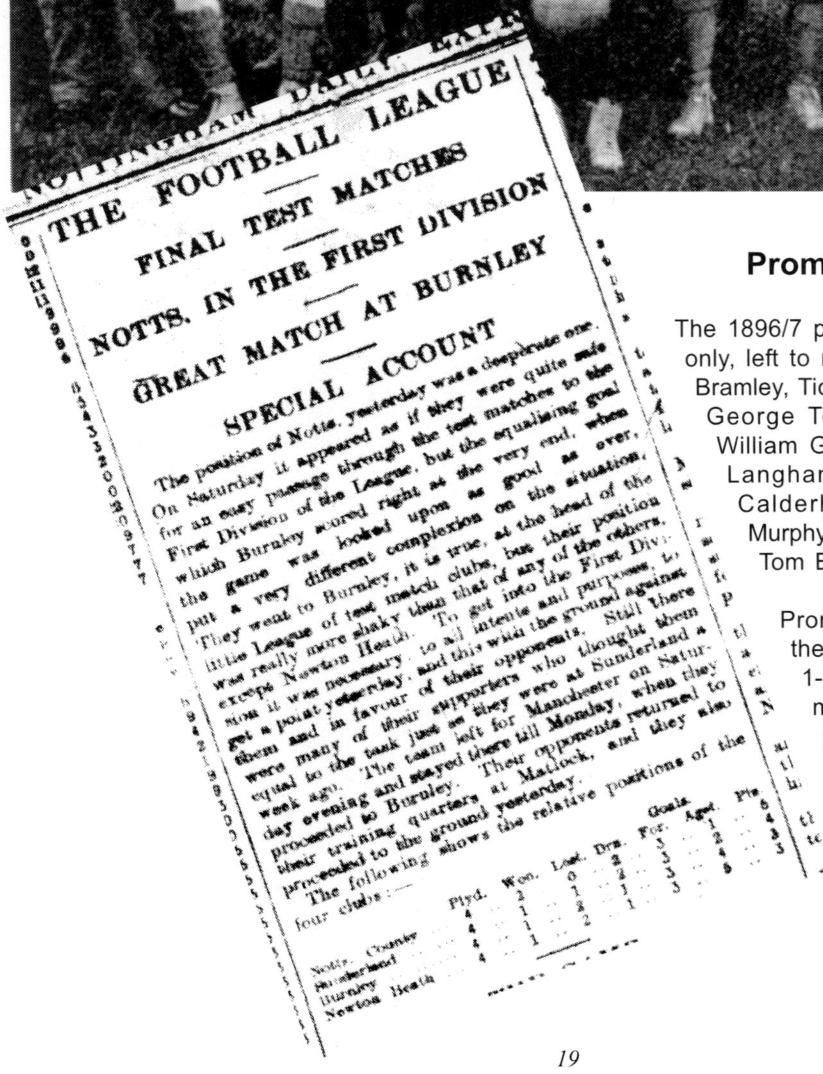

NOTTINGHAM DAILY EXPRESS

THE FOOTBALL LEAGUE

FINAL TEST MATCHES

NOTTS. IN THE FIRST DIVISION

GREAT MATCH AT BURNLEY

SPECIAL ACCOUNT

The position of Notts. yesterday was a desperate one. On Saturday it appeared as if they were quite safe for an easy passage through the test matches to the First Division of the League, but the equalising goal which Burnley scored right at the very end, when the game was looked upon as good as over, put a very different complexion on the situation. They went to Burnley, it is true, at the head of the little League of test match clubs, but their position was really more shaky than that of any of the others, except Newton Heath. To get into the First Division it was necessary, to all intents and purposes, to get a point yesterday, and this with the ground against them and in favour of their opponents. Still there were many of their supporters who thought them equal to the task just as they were at Sunderland a week ago. The team left for Manchester on Saturday evening and stayed there till Monday, when they proceeded to Burnley. Their opponents returned to their training quarters at Matlock, and they also proceeded to the ground yesterday.

The following shows the relative positions of the four clubs:—

	Plyd.	Won.	Lost.	Drn.	Goals For.	Goals Agst.	Pts.
Notts. County	4	2	0	2	3	1	6
Sunderland	4	1	1	2	3	2	4
Burnley	4	1	2	1	3	4	3
Newton Heath	4	1	2	1	3	5	3

Promotion 1896/7

The 1896/7 promotion side. Players only, left to right: Standing: Charlie Bramley, Tich Smith, Tom Prescott, George Toone, Elijah Allsopp, William Gibson. Sitting: William Langham, John Allan, David Calderhead (in suit), John Murphy, Walter Bull. On ground: Tom Boucher.

Promotion was secured in the last 'test' match with a 1-0 victory at Burnley. Test matches were a kind of play-off mini-league and were replaced by automatic promotion and relegation from 1898/9.

3: Football at Trent Bridge

Main Events

1867-83 Home games were played occasionally at Trent Bridge in these years but the most regular venues were the Meadows Cricket Ground and later the Castle Cricket Ground.

1883-1910 Most of Notts County's home matches were played at Trent Bridge from 1883/4 until 1909/10. When Trent Bridge was needed for cricket, Notts played their home games at the Castle Cricket Ground (until 1894) and then on Nottingham Forest's grounds – the Town Ground (1895 and 1896) and the City Ground (1899 to 1909).

The view towards the Pavilion, which was erected in 1887.

The view towards what is now Radcliffe Road (behind the far goal) and Fox Road (behind the right side of the ground).

Cricket Ground

The1899/00 team group in front of the Pavilion. (l to r): Standing: William Bramley (Treasurer), Tom Harris (Secretary), Tom Prescott, Ernest Suter, George Lewis, Billy Ball, Alf Shelton (Director), Joe Goode (Trainer). Sitting: Arthur Hadley, Alex Maconnachie, David Calderhead, Harry Fletcher, James Chalmers, Jimmy Thomas (Director). On ground: Walter Bull, Joe McMain.

A team group taken at the Radcliffe Road end in 1905-06. (l to r): Jerry Dean, Percy Humphreys, Harry Mainman, Arthur Green, Teddy Emberton, Matt Reilly, Arthur Griffiths, Walter Tarplin, Jack Montgomery, Ben Craythorne, Ellis Gee.

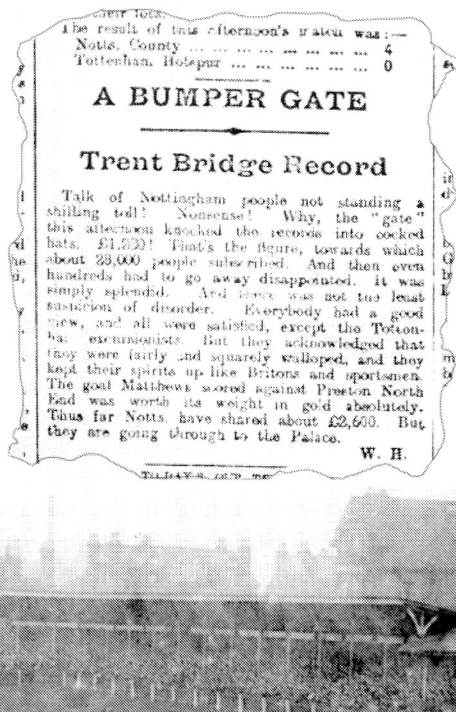

The result of this afternoon's match was:—

Notts. County	4
Tottenham Hotspur	0

A BUMPER GATE

Trent Bridge Record

Talk of Nottingham people not standing a shilling toll! Nonsense! Why, the "gate" this afternoon knocked the records into cocked hats. £1,230! That's the figure, towards which about 28,000 people subscribed. And then even hundreds had to go away disappointed. It was simply splendid. And there was not the least suspicion of disorder. Everybody had a good view, and all were satisfied, except the Tottenham excursionists. But they acknowledged that they were fairly and squarely walloped, and they kept their spirits up like Britons and sportsmen. The goal Matthews scored against Preston North End was worth its weight in gold absolutely. Thus far Notts. have shared about £2,600. But they are going through to the Palace.

W. H.

Admission prices were doubled for the FA Cup tie against Tottenham Hotspur on 23 February 1907. It was the record gate for Trent Bridge in financial terms and also the record crowd if the estimate of 28,000 was accurate.

Action from the last game at Trent Bridge, on 16 April 1910 against Aston Villa.

4: Into the 20th Century: 1900/01 to 1914/15

Main Events

1900/01 Notts equalled their best-ever League performance – third in Division 1.

1910 Moved to Meadow Lane.

1912/13 Relegated to Division 2.

1913/14 Promoted to Division 1. Champions of Division 2.

(League football was suspended from 1915/16 to1918/19 because of the First World War)

(Above) The 1900/01 side that finished third in Division 1, the highest position achieved in the 20th century:
Standing (l to r): William Bramley (Treasurer), Tom Prescott, Tom Harris (Secretary), Harry Pennington, Spencer (Director), George Lewis, Callan (Director). Sitting: Alex Maconnachie, Billy Ball, Walter Bull, Ted McDonald, Jack Montgomery. On ground: Arthur Hadley, Alf Warner, Billy Ross, Jack Morris, Ellis Gee. Joe Goode (Trainer).

Albert Iremonger, the legendary goalkeeper, played a club record 601 League and FA Cup matches from 1905 to 1926. His height of 6ft 5inches made him a commanding figure on the pitch and his eccentric character endeared him to supporters but possibly cost him a place in the England side.

This 1903/4 team group includes Herbert Chapman, later to become the legendary trophy-winning manager of Huddersfield and Arsenal in the 1920s and 1930s. He played 7 games for Notts. Back (l to r): Herbert Dainty, Jack Montgomery, Ted McDonald, ? . Standing: ?, Tom Prescott, Tom Harris (Secretary), Harry Mainman, Arthur Griffiths, William Ross, Walter Bull, ?, Ellis Gee, G. Swift (Trainer), Percy Humphreys. Sitting: Herbert Chapman, ? , Arthur Green, Harry Pennington, ? ,?

Notable Players

Over 50 goals – Jimmy Cantrell, Jerry Dean, Arthur Green, Percy Humphreys, Jack Peart, Sam Richards .

Over 200 appearances – Arthur Clamp, Jerry Dean, Teddy Emberton, Ellis Gee, Percy Humphreys, Albert Iremonger, Billy Flint, Jack Montgomery, Bert Morley and Tom Prescott. Billy Flint's 200 appearances spanned the periods before and after the First World War.

Internationals – Percy Humphreys, Bert Morley (both played for England); Arthur Green (Wales)

Others – Ben Craythorne, Herbert Chapman.

NOTTS COUNTY'S NEW GROUND.

Views of Meadow Lane in August 1910, a few days before the first-ever game was played there. The Meadow Lane stand was transferred from Trent Bridge and reconstructed at the new stadium.

The move to Meadow Lane

The first County Road stand, which was replaced in1925 by the more familiar gabled stand.

(Right) An extract from the programme for the first match at Meadow Lane on 3 September 1910 against Nottingham Forest.

Don't forget to

KEEP THIS PROGRAMME

AS

A SOUVENIR

OF

THE FIRST MATCH

ON THE NEW

'COUNTY' GROUND

Saturday, Sept. 3, 1910.

———o———

Our Own Home at Last.

Notts. have at last made the plunge and opened out a new ground on their own.

This will be decidedly to their advantage as now they will be able to do exactly as they like in the way of arrangements.

It must have required years of thought and worry before finally deciding, as of course thousands of pounds do not grow on plum trees.

(Below) The staff who made the transition from Trent Bridge to Meadow Lane in 1910. Standing (l to r): William Bramley (Treasurer), Teddy Emberton, Tom Harris (Secretary), Bert Morley, Albert Iremonger, Ernest Suter, Arthur Clamp, Arthur Griffiths, Tom Prescott (Trainer), Tom McLean (Asst. Trainer). Sitting: Ben Craythorne, Jerry Dean, Bill Matthews, Jack Montgomery, Jimmy Cantrell, George Dodd, Albert Walker. On ground: Ike Waterall, Fred Jones, Andrew Mosley.

Overseas tour

The Magpies first tour abroad was for 3 games in Denmark in June1910. The line-up for this game in Copenhagen was (l to r, players only): Standing: Jimmy Cantrell, Albert Iremonger, Arthur Clamp, Alf Griffiths. Sitting: Teddy Emberton, Jerry Dean, Bill Matthews, Ben Craythorne, Fred Jones, George Dodd, Birch.

Notts played 3 games in Spain in1914, all against Barcelona. They won all three matches, one of them 10-3 after being 2-1 down at half-time.

Promotion 1913/14

The champions of Division 2 in1913/14.
Standing (l to r): Tom McLean (Asst. Trainer), J. Tuke, Arthur Clamp, Albert Iremonger, Murray Steele, Teddy Emberton, Jack Peart, Ike Waterall, Tom Prescott (Trainer).
Sitting: Richard Allsebrook, Ted Bassett, Billy Flint, Sam Richards, Bert Morley, Alf West, Bill Jennings, Horace Henshall, Joe Perry. On ground: George Dale, John Lamb.

Promotion to Division 1 was secured at Barnsley on 4 April 1914.

A souvenir of the banquet held to celebrate the 1913/14 season promotion.

Three of the star players of the era

1: (Left) Centre-forward **Jimmy Cantrell** scored 65 League and Cup goals in 136 games from 1908 to 1912. He was sold to Tottenham Hotspur and played in their FA Cup Final victory in 1921.

2: (Lower left) **Arthur Clamp** was the club's regular centre-half from 1907 to 1915, playing 389 times and going for long spells without missing a game. He died in September 1918 from wounds received in the First World War and was honoured by thousands of people who lined the streets for his funeral procession in Nottingham.

3: (Right) **Jack Peart** was signed from Newcastle United and followed Cantrell as the regular centre-forward. He scored 52 League and Cup goals in 84 appearances between1912 and 1919.

5: Late Iremonger Era: 1919/20 to 1925/6

Main Events

1919/20 Relegated to Division 2.
1920/1 New attendance record.
1921/2 Reached FA Cup semi-final.
1922/3 Promoted to Division 1. Champions of Division 2.
1924/5 Finished 9th in Division 1 after topping the table earlier in the season. Never bettered since.
1925 New County Road stand erected.
1925/6 Relegated to Division 2. It would take 55 years to return to Division 1.

Notable Players

Over 50 goals – Arthur Davis, Harold Hill.
Over 200 appearances – Bill Ashurst, Norman Dinsdale, Billy Flint, Albert Iremonger, Haydn Kemp.
International – Bill Ashurst (England).
Others – Donald Cock, Horace Cope

The 1922 Semi-Final

Notts reached the FA Cup semi-final in 1922 after each of the preceding 4 rounds went to replays – a total of 10 games. They lost 3-1 in the semi-final to Huddersfield Town, then managed by Herbert Chapman. The match was played at Turf Moor, Burnley.

(Above) Albert Iremonger is beaten for Huddersfield's first goal as Bill Ashurst looks on.

Billy Flint leads County out; Notts attack the Huddersfield goal. The Magpies team was Iremonger, Ashurst, Marriott, Flint, Dinsdale, Kemp, Daly, Cook, Widdowson, Hill, Henshall.

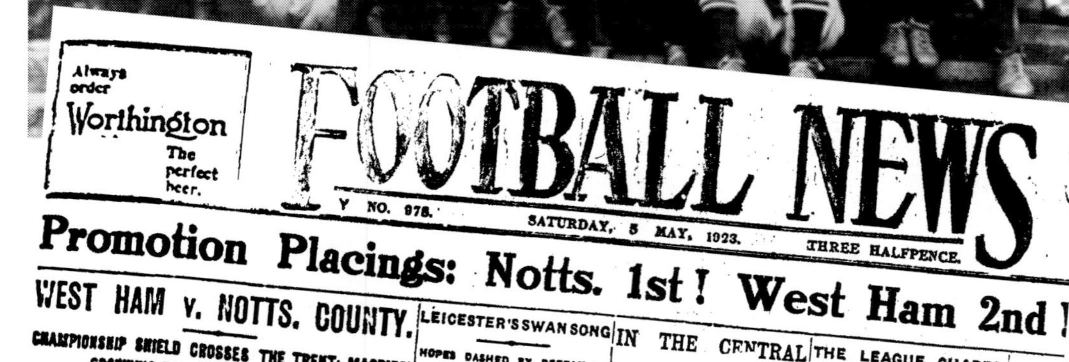

Always order Worthington The perfect beer.

FOOTBALL NEWS

No. 978. SATURDAY, 5 MAY, 1923. THREE HALFPENCE.

Promotion Placings: Notts. 1st! West Ham 2nd!

WEST HAM v. NOTTS. COUNTY.

CHAMPIONSHIP SHIELD CROSSES THE TRENT: MAGPIES' CROWNING TRIUMPH AT UPTON PARK.

LEICESTER'S SWAN SONG

HOPES DASHED BY DEFEAT

IN THE CENTRAL

THE LEAGUE CHARTS.

HOW THE CLUBS STAND AFTER TO-DAY'S GAMES.

FIRST LEAGUE.

SECOND LEAGUE.

Top: The champions of Division 2 for 1922/3. Back: Lachlan McPherson, Charlie Bell (Coach), Horace Cope, Jimmy Iremonger (Trainer), Bob Platts, Frank Marriott, Jack Cook, James Heathcote, Albert Iremonger, Bill Ashurst, Tom McLean (Asst. Trainer), Billy Death. Sitting: Joe Daly, Alf Widdowson, Billy Flint, Harold Hill, Norman Dinsdale, Jack Wren, Tom Gibson, Bert Ashford, George Harris. Front: E. Shepherd, A. Kirkwood.

On the last day of the season, Notts, West Ham and Leicester all started the day on 51 points but Notts' magnificent away win at West Ham sent them up as champions of Division 2.

Norman Dinsdale and goalkeeper George Streets in action at Stockport. Billy Flint is in the background.

The 1924/5 team. Standing (l to r): Albert Fisher (Manager), Jack Wren, Jimmy Iremonger (Trainer), Bill Ashurst, Norman Dinsdale, Albert Iremonger, Llew Price, Tom McLean (Asst. Trainer). Sitting: Arthur Davis, Len Barry, Harold Hill, Billy Flint, Haydn Kemp, Alf Widdowson, Ralph Cornwall, Horace Cope. On ground: Bob Platts, Joe Daly, Donald Cock.

Top of the First Division

LEAGUE RESULTS AND TABLES.

THE CHAMPIONSHIP.

	Goals.		Goals.
NOTTS COUNTY .. .. (Cock)	1	ARSENAL	0
*ASTON VILLA .. .. (Kirton, Walker)	2	BOLTON WANDERERS .. (John Smith, Joe Smith)	2
*BLACKBURN ROVERS .. (McCleery)	1	WEST BROMWICH ALBION	0
*BURY .. .. .. (Robbie, Ball 2)	3	SUNDERLAND	0
TOTTENHAM HOTSPUR .. (Seed, Thompson)	2	HUDDERSFIELD TOWN (C. Wilson)	1
*LIVERPOOL .. .. (Rawlings, Forshaw 2)	3	PRESTON NORTH END .. (Harrison)	1
*MANCHESTER CITY .. (Austin, Roberts)	2	EVERTON .. .. (Chadwick 2)	2
*NEWCASTLE UNITED .. (Cowan, Clarke 2)	3	BURNLEY	0
*NOTTINGHAM FOREST .. (Burton, Flood)	2	CARDIFF CITY .. .. (Beadles)	1
*SHEFFIELD UNITED .. (Tunstall)	1	LEEDS UNITED .. (Swann)	1
BIRMINGHAM .. .. (Bradford)	1	WEST HAM UNITED	0

	P.	W.	D.	L.	Goals. F.	Goals. A.	Pts.
Notts County	14	8	3	3	16	7	19
Birmingham	14	8	3	3	13	12	19
West Bromwich Albion	14	7	3	4	15	10	17
Bury	14	5	7	2	21	18	17
Sunderland	13	7	2	4	24	15	16
Newcastle United ..	15	4	8	3	22	16	16
Aston Villa	14	4	8	2	24	19	16
Blackburn Rovers ..	15	5	6	4	21	20	16
Huddersfield Town ..	13	5	5	3	17	9	15
Liverpool	12	6	3	3	22	15	15
Manchester City	14	6	3	5	29	23	15
Leeds United	14	5	5	4	17	16	15
Bolton Wanderers ..	13	4	6	3	24	19	14
Arsenal	14	6	2	6	13	16	14
West Ham United ..	14	4	5	5	12	15	13
Tottenham Hotspur ..	14	4	4	6	14	15	12
Everton	14	3	6	5	13	17	12
Cardiff City	13	4	3	6	16	16	11
Nottingham Forest ..	14	4	2	8	12	23	10
Sheffield United	14	2	5	7	15	25	9
Burnley	13	1	6	6	9	17	8
Preston North End ..	13	1	1	11	5	30	3

In 1924/5 Notts went to the top of the First Division after beating Manchester City on 1 November and stayed there with a victory against Arsenal at Highbury on 8 November. They drew the next 3 matches and were knocked off the top by a 3-0 defeat at West Ham on 6 December.

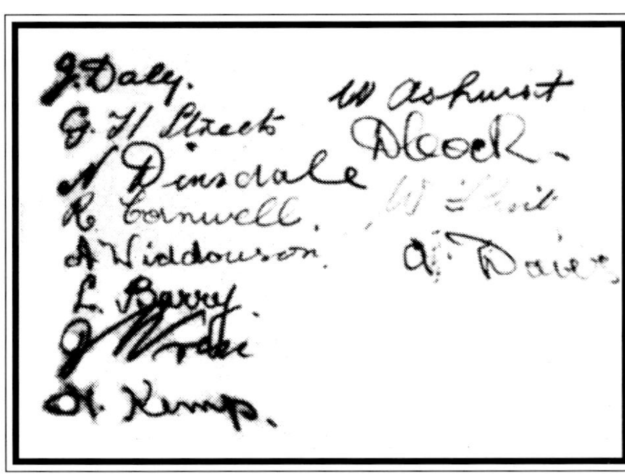

Autographs of the side that took Notts to the top of the First Division.

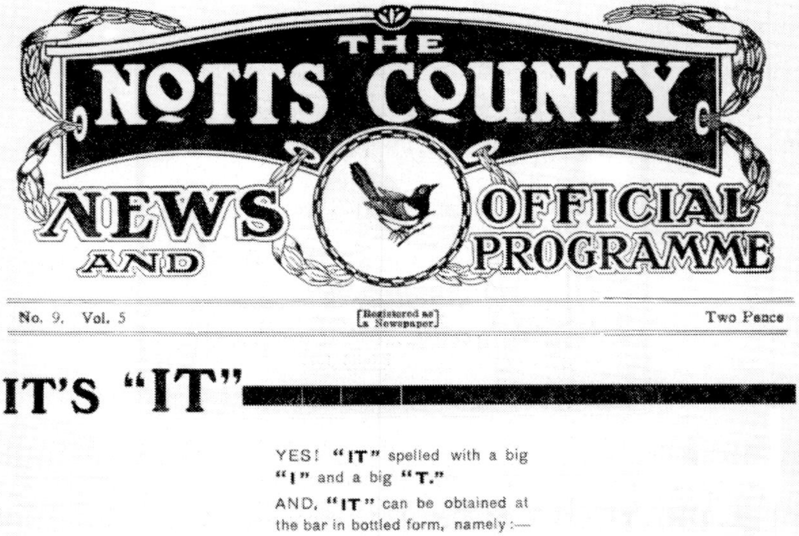
THE NOTTS COUNTY NEWS AND OFFICIAL PROGRAMME

No. 9. Vol. 5 [Registered as a Newspaper] Two Pence

IT'S "IT"

YES! "IT" spelled with a big "I" and a big "T."

AND, "IT" can be obtained at the bar in bottled form, namely :—

The Magpie badge worn on the players' shirts during the 3 First Division seasons 1923-1926.

The header of the programme cover for the First Division match against Sheffield United in 1924/5.

The Meadow Lane Ground

A new County Road stand, the one with the familiar gable, was built for the start of the 1925/6 season. Although this photograph was taken in 1949 it shows how the stands at Meadow Lane looked from 1925 until1978.

An aerial photo of Meadow Lane taken in the mid-1920s, after the construction of the new County Road stand. There were houses in the vicinity of the ground until the 1960s.

Trips abroad

(Above)County visited Spain for the second time in 1922. As well as playing Scottish club St. Mirren there, they played twice against Barcelona. The photograph shows the side for one of the games against Barcelona. Players only, l to r. Standing: Norman Dinsdale, George Streets, Lachlan McPherson, Billy Death, Tom Gibson. On ground: Haydn Kemp, Bob Platts, Horace Cope (kneeling), Bill Ashurst, Jack Cook, Frank Marriott.

(Below) In the summer of1925 Notts toured central Europe, with games in Vienna and Prague. This was the team that played in Prague on 11 May. Players only. Back (l to r): George Smith, Haydn Kemp, Alf Widdowson, George Streets, Jack Wren, Arthur Davis, Ralph Cornwall. Front: Norman Dinsdale, Len Barry, Chris Staniforth, Joe Daly.

Three of the star players of the era

Bill Ashurst, right-back, played 222 games from 1920 to 1926 and appeared 5 times for England.

Donald Cock, centre-forward, scored 34 goals in 92 games between 1922 and 1925 before he was sold to Arsenal.

At the age of 42, after more than 20 years sterling service and 601 appearances, **Albert Iremonger** was transferred to Lincoln City at the end of the 1925/6 season. Supporters felt that he still had more to offer and that he was sold too soon. A road near the ground is named after him.

6: Down the Ladder: 1926/7 to 1938/9

Main Events

1928/9	5th in Division 2.
1929/30	Relegated to Division 3 (South) for the first time.
1930/1	Promoted to Division 2. Champions of Division 3 (South).
1934/5	Relegated to Division 3 (South).
1936/7	Finished 2nd and narrowly missed promotion.

Notable Players

Over 50 goals – Harold Andrews, Tom Fenner, Tom Keetley.

Over 200 appearances – Charlie Bisby, Bill Corkhill, Alf Feebery, Sam Haden, Percy Mills, George Taylor.

Internationals – Willie Davies, Eddie Lawrence (both played for Wales); Bill Fallon, Con Moulson (both played for the Irish Republic).

Others – Hughie Gallagher, 'Boy' Martin, 'Dixie' Dean, Willie Hall.

The 1928/9 side that finished 5th in Division 2. Standing (l to r): Joe Astley, Percy Mills, Tom Ratcliffe (Trainer), Jimmy Ferguson, Fred Hilton, Syd Plackett, Charlie Bisby. Sitting: Willie Davies, Tom Fenner, George Taylor, Harold Andrews, Sam Haden. On ground: Haydn Kemp, Bertie 'Paddy' Mills.

Promotion 1930/1

The Third Division (South) Championship shield and medals being presented to Notts by Charles Sutcliffe, president of the Football League.

(Right) Trainer Fred Banks, second left, with four of the 1930/1 promotion team. The players, left to right, are Percy Mills, Harold Andrews, Tom Keetley and Charlie Bisby.

(Left) The 1930/1 squad that won the Division 3 (South) Championship. Standing (l to r): Billy Hamilton, Fred Banks (Trainer), Frank Froggatt, George Turner, Jimmy Ferguson, Harold Wightman (Coach), Harry Soutar, Harold Smith, Percy Mills, Horace Henshall (Manager), George Stimpson. Sitting: Tom Fenner, Alf Feebery, Charlie Bisby, Haydn Kemp, Tom Keetley, Harold Andrews, Sam Haden, Harry Lovatt. On ground: George Jakeman, George Taylor, Arthur Maw, Francis Shooter, Jack Dowsey.

The match against Northampton on 22 November attracted a crowd of 21,329, the biggest of the 1930/1 promotion season. Harold Andrews is challenging the Northampton goalkeeper, with Tom Keetley on the left.

Centre-forward Tom Keetley holds the club record for the most League goals scored in one season, with 39 in 1930/1. He scored a total of 98 League and Cup goals in 110 games from 1929 to 1933, and holds the distinction of scoring hat-tricks in three consecutive away matches in 1931/2.

Notts. County's Recor

CHESTERFIELD V. NOTTS. COUNTY

KEETLEY'S HAT TRICK AND 250TH GOAL IN LEAGUE FOOTBALL

THIRD DIVISION CHAMPIONS CLASH UNDER SHADOW OF THE CROOKED SPIRE.

MAGPIES WELL ON TOP

THE Third Division Champions of last season met for the first time in a League match at Chesterfield to-day.

With Notts. County's cup-tie triumph

other gruelling time dealing with a swift Notts. attack.

Luck at Last.

Keetley almost scored with a remarkable overhead kick, Ashmore sav-

Billy or Willie Hall was a highly talented inside-left who started his career at Notts with 35 games in 1931 and 1932. His sale to Tottenham Hotspur caused outrage with supporters. He later played 10 games for England.

The mid-30s

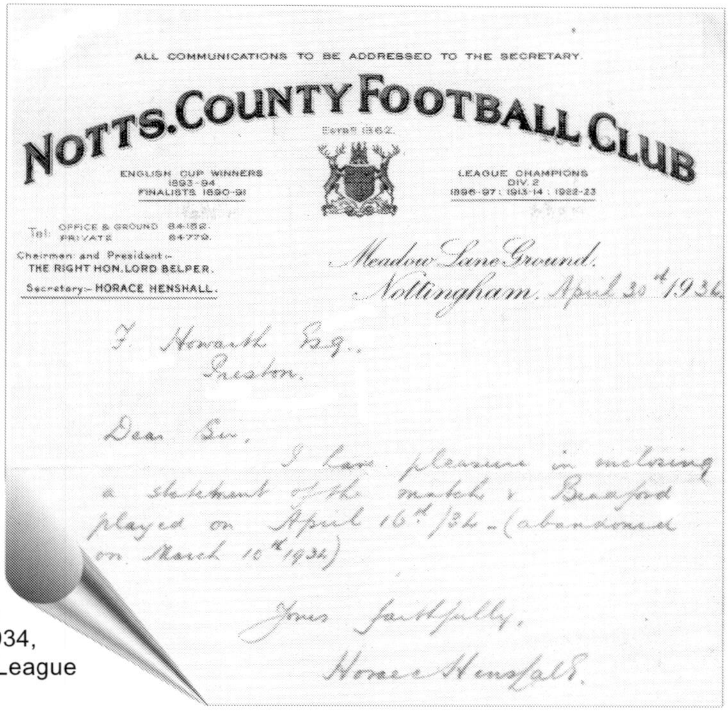

ALL COMMUNICATIONS TO BE ADDRESSED TO THE SECRETARY.

NOTTS. COUNTY FOOTBALL CLUB

Estab 1862.

ENGLISH CUP WINNERS 1893-94 FINALISTS 1890-91

LEAGUE CHAMPIONS DIV. 2 1896-97 : 1913-14 : 1922-23

Tel: OFFICE & GROUND 84182. PRIVATE 84779.

Chairman and President:- THE RIGHT HON. LORD BELPER.

Secretary:- HORACE HENSHALL.

Meadow Lane Ground.
Nottingham. April 30th 1934

F. Howarth Esq.,
Preston.

Dear Sir,

I have pleasure in enclosing a statement of the match v Brentford played on April 16th /34 - (abandoned on March 10th 1934)

Yours faithfully,

Horace Henshall.

A letter from Horace Henshall, an ex-player and County's secretary-manager from June 1927 until May 1934, written to the Football League about gate receipts.

Notts changed their colours back to chocolate and blue halves for one season in 1934/5 but reverted to black and white stripes after being relegated.
This is the team that played at Oldham on 8 September 1934 (l to r):
Back: George Walker, Bill Corkhill, Percy Mills, Tommy Knox, Alf Feebery, Eddie Lawrence.
Front: Jimmy McGrath, Tex Rickards, Charlie Macartney, Johnny Rankin, Sam Haden.

The Notts players at the start of the 1936/7 season. Further quality was added in September with the signings of Hughie Gallacher and Con Moulson and the Magpies mounted a serious challenge for promotion which only failed in the last couple of matches. Back (l to r): Wyness, Kavanagh, Chalmers, Blyth, Shaw, Vasey, Millington. Standing: Ratcliffe (Trainer), Julian, Mills, Feebery, Corkhill, Lowery, Walker, Rickards, Haden (Asst. Trainer). Sitting: J. Smith, P. Smith (Secretary-Manager), Hobson (Director), Walker (Director), Barnes (Chairman), Towers (Director), Phillip (Director), Fallon. On ground: Ferguson, Taylor, Stevens, Flewitt, Mardon.

GALLACHER'S ARTISTRY A DELIGHT

Famous Scot Captains Notts. in First Match

ATTENDANCE DOUBLED

GOAL SCORERS.

Mins.	Scorer.	Score.
72	**Chalmers** (Notts. Co.)	1—0
85	**Fallon** (Notts. Co.)	2—0

THE presence of Hughie Gallacher in Notts. County's ranks, as expected, made the turnstiles at Meadow-lane more busily than they have been doing.

The introduction of the famous Scot and the substitution of Shaw for Rickards, was the only change in the teams, which fielded as follows before 12,000 spectators.

To the delight of the crowd it was noticed that Gallacher had taken over the captaincy of the side. Teams:—

NOTTS. COUNTY		TORQUAY UNITED
Blyth	goal	Maggs
Mills	right back	Green
Feebury	left back	Parker
Corkhill	right half-back	Hutchinson
Wyness	centre half-back	Jones
Vasey	left half-back	Llewellyn
Millington	outside right	Johnson
Chalmers	inside right	Philbin
Gallacher	centre forward	Morton
Shaw	inside left	Beedall
Fallon	outside left	Morgan

Referee: Mr. F. W. Wort (London).

HUGH GALLACHER.

The Game

Gallacher [illegible] the toss, and Notts. were set to face a slight breeze; but they were the first to be aggressive.

Their left wing was very active, but the Torquay defence was resolute and avoided real danger to their goal.

In their first breakaway, the Torquay attack worked skilfully and Beedall [illegible] them, and FALLON had little difficulty in beating Maggs.

(Right) **Hughie Gallacher** runs onto the Meadow Lane pitch for his debut on 26 September 1936 against Torquay United. 16,021 saw the game compared with crowds of 5,000 and 7,000 for the previous two.

(Below) Centre-half **Con Moulson** joined Notts from Lincoln City at the same time as Gallacher and added strength to the defence. He played twice for the Irish Republic whilst with the Magpies.

(Right) **'Dixie' Dean**, who made his name with Everton and England, was another legendary centre-forward who came to Meadow Lane late in his career. He had lost his place in the Everton side to the young Tommy Lawton. A broken bone in his foot restricted him to 9 appearances and 3 goals for Notts between March and November 1938.

(Opposite page, bottom right) **Hughie Gallacher** had achieved fame as a great but temperamental centre-forward with Newcastle, Chelsea and Scotland since the late 1920s. He joined Notts from Derby County early in 1936-7 and played a major part in the push for promotion that season. He scored 32 goals in 46 games in 1936/7 and 1937/8 before deciding to move on.

7: Wartime: 1939/40 to 1945/6

Main Events

1939-46 The League was suspended and football was organised into regional league and cup competitions, with clubs allowed to field guest players.

1941/2 Only one game was played at Meadow Lane as a result of bomb damage in May 1941.

1945/6 In preparation for the resumption of League football in 1946/7, fixtures were regionalised but based on the pre-war League structure. Notts were one of 11 teams in the Third Division South (Northern Section).

Notable Players

Guests – Sam Bartram (Charlton), Bernard Streten (Luton), Tommy Lawton (Everton), Sammy Crooks (Derby), Dally Duncan (Derby), Frank Broome (Derby), Cyril Sidlow (Liverpool), Andy Beattie (Preston), Leon Leuty (Derby), Gordon Bradley (Leicester).

Own players - Jesse Pye, Ian McPherson.

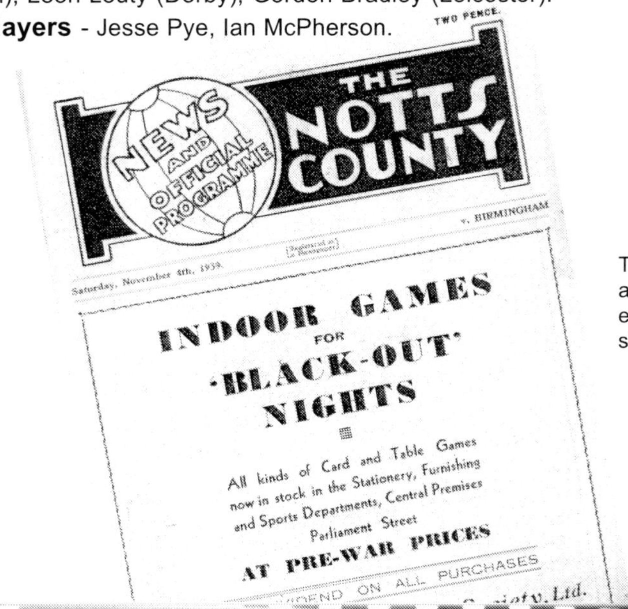

The reference to black-outs in the advertisement on the cover of this early wartime programme was a sign of the times.

Meadow Lane was hit by German bombs in a raid on Nottingham on the night of 8/9 May 1941.

Wartime action against Nottingham Forest

A simple but effective message replaced the usual advertisement in this late wartime programme – the 'V' denotes 'Victory in Europe'.

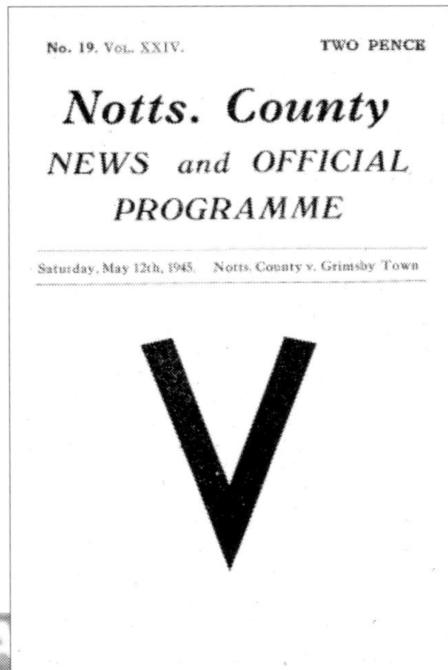

No. 19. Vol. XXIV. TWO PENCE

Notts. County

NEWS and OFFICIAL PROGRAMME

Saturday, May 12th, 1945. Notts. County v. Grimsby Town

V

German prisoners clearing snow from the pitch in the mid-1940s

A 1945/6 team group. Back (l to r): Robert Allen, P.C. Ratcliffe, Harry Brown, Aubrey Southwell, J. Sheen. Front: Reg Beresford, Jesse Pye, Ian McPherson, Albert Parks, R.D. Meredith, Bill Corkhill.

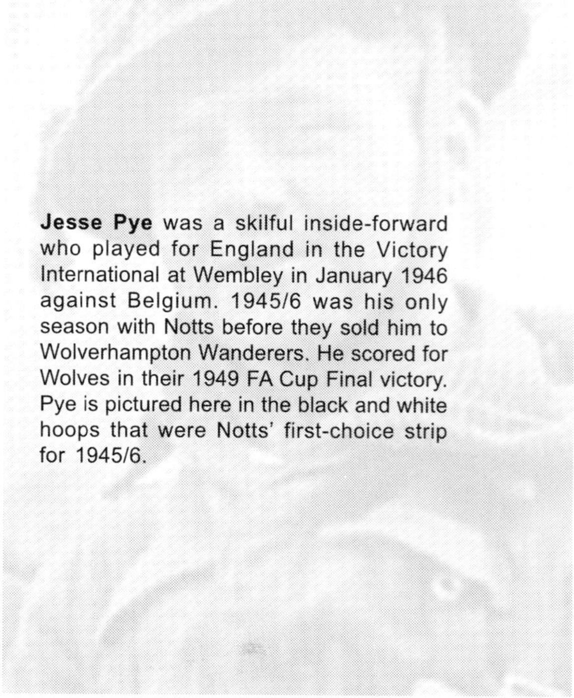

Jesse Pye was a skilful inside-forward who played for England in the Victory International at Wembley in January 1946 against Belgium. 1945/6 was his only season with Notts before they sold him to Wolverhampton Wanderers. He scored for Wolves in their 1949 FA Cup Final victory. Pye is pictured here in the black and white hoops that were Notts' first-choice strip for 1945/6.

8: Lawton & A Golden Era: 1946/7 to 1954/5

Main Events

1947/8 Tommy Lawton signed for a British record fee.

1947-55 The average home crowd for each of these 8 seasons comes in the top 8 of the club's entire history. Many individual attendances over 30,000 and 40,000.

1949/50 Promoted to Division 2. Champions of Division 3 (South). All-time record home League crowd. The average home crowd of 34,659 remains the all-time highest for either Nottingham club (Nottingham Forest's best was 32,715 in 1967/8).

1950/1 Jackie Sewell sold for another British record fee.

1951/2 Lawton sold.

1954/5 7th in Division 2 - best League position since 1928/9. Reached round 6 of the FA Cup. All-time record attendance for any Notts home match. Reserve side were champions of the Midland League.

Notable Players

Over 50 goals – Tommy Lawton, Jackie Sewell, Tom Johnston, Jimmy Jackson.

Over 200 appearances – Harry Adamson, Gordon Bradley, Tommy Deans, Tom Johnston, Leon Leuty, Aubrey Southwell, Ron Wylie.

Internationals – Tommy Lawton (England), Eddie Gannon (Irish Republic).

Tommy Lawton – Notts County's greatest player and also regarded by many who saw him play as England's greatest centre-forward. It caused a sensation when he was transferred from Chelsea in November 1947 in a deal worth £20,000, a new British record fee. His power and skill with both head and feet made him a huge crowd-puller and a hero with the enthusiastic public.

His goal-scoring achievements with Everton and England were legend and he made 4 more appearances for his country while Notts were in Division 3 (South). He led the Magpies to promotion in 1949/50 and scored 103 League and Cup goals in 166 appearances.

Lawton rises above a defender to get in a header against QPR in 1950/1.

Lawton demonstrates his powerful shooting technique.

Tommy races in to score one of his many goals for Notts.

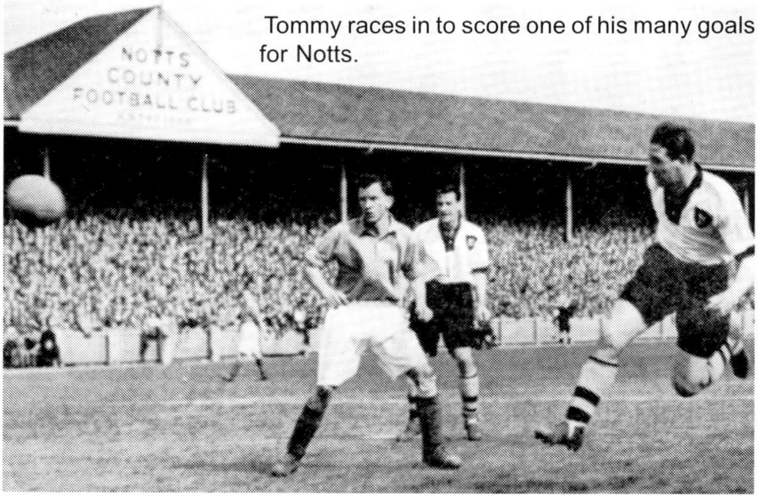

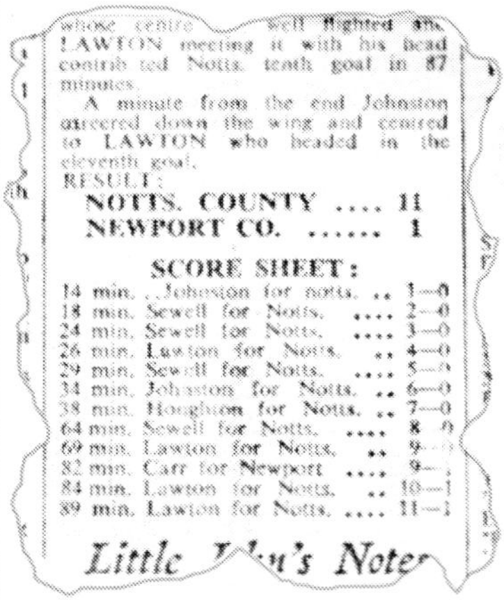

whose centre ... well flighted and LAWTON meeting it with his head contributed Notts. tenth goal in 87 minutes.

A minute from the end Johnston steered down the wing and centred to LAWTON who headed in the eleventh goal.

RESULT:

NOTTS. COUNTY 11
NEWPORT CO. 1

SCORE SHEET:

14 min. ..Johnston for notts. .. 1—0
18 min. Sewell for Notts. .... 2—0
24 min. Sewell for Notts. .... 3—0
26 min. Lawton for Notts. .. 4—0
29 min. Sewell for Notts. .... 5—0
34 min. Johnston for Notts. .. 6—0
38 min. Houghton for Notts. .. 7—0
64 min. Sewell for Notts. .... 8—0
69 min. Lawton for Notts. .. 9—0
82 min. Carr for Newport .... 9—1
84 min. Lawton for Notts. .. 10—1
89 min. Lawton for Notts. .... 11—1

Little J...n's Note...

The famous 11-1 win over Newport County on 15 January 1949 is the Magpies' record League victory.

A 1948/9 team group (l to r): Back: Eddie Gannon, Aubrey Southwell, Harry Brown, Norman Rigby, Billy Baxter. Front: Tony Freeman, Jackie Sewell, Tommy Lawton, Jackie Marsh, Tom Johnston, Bill Corkhill.

The crowds

(Above) Enthusiastic supporters on the way to Plymouth to see Notts beat Argyle 1-0 in a 3rd round FA Cup tie on 8 January 1949. The Magpies lost 1-0 at Liverpool in the next round in front of 61,003 spectators, the biggest-ever crowd for any Notts match.

(Above) The Main stand side of Meadow Lane is full as usual for the game against Preston in 1950/1.

(Right)There are no empty spaces on Spion Kop as Alex Simpson is backed up by Jackie Sewell near the Preston goal on 23 September 1950.

Spectators in the packed County Road stand watch Lawton and Sewell on the attack against Blackburn on 11 November 1950.

Promotion 1949/50

The 1949/50 promotion side (left to right): Standing: Billy Baxter, Tommy Deans, Aubrey Southwell, Roy Smith, Eric Houghton (Manager), Norman Rigby, Harry Chapman, Harry Adamson. Sitting: Frank Broome, Jackie Sewell, Tommy Lawton, Bill Evans, Tom Johnston. On ground: Fred Evans, Alex Simpson.

Lawton has just scored with a typical bullet-like header in the 2-1 away victory at Nottingham Forest on 3 December 1949.

Jackie Sewell, Charlie Barnes (Chairman) and Tommy Lawton with the Division 3 (South) championship shield.

THEIR FIRST DOUBLE OVER REDS

46,000 People See Sewell and Lawton Score

AT Meadow Lane this afternoon, the attendance record went by the board easily, all the 46,000 tickets issued for the Notts. County and Forest return fixture having been disposed of.

Grand weather prevailed when Forest won the toss. They lacked Gager, for whom Rawson again deputised at centre-half. Lawton, despite a cold, led the home attack.

The police controlled the entrance of the crowd by the means of loud-speakers.

Some of the younger supporters of both sides had assembled at the gates as early as 9.30 a.m.

It was a very orderly crowd, and there was considerable enthusiasm concerning this local Derby, which meant so much to Notts, County in their promotion aspirations.

They were at full strength and relied on the players who had taken them to the top of the Southern Section in the early stages of the season.

It was unfortunate for the Forest that Gager was still unfit, and his place at centre-half was taken by Rawson, who had played since the Easter match against Bristol Rovers at Eastville.

Lawton's cold did not keep him out of the leadership of the home attack.

Notts. County. — Smith; Deans, Rigby; Chapman, Baxter, Adamson; Broome, Sewell, Lawton, Evans (W.), Johnston.

Nottingham Forest. — Walker; Whare, McCall; Anderson, Rawson, Morley; Scott, Love, Ardron, Capel, Kaile.

Referee: J. W. Topliss, Grimsby

Forest won the toss and played towards the Meadow Lane goal.

The County made two early advances and when the ball came over from Broome, Walker dangerously left his goal, but was fortunate that he was in the way of a shot from Lawton.

Then Love looked like getting the better of Baxter inside the penalty [illegible] was [illegible] dispossess[illegible] keeper came to meet him and beat him in the race.

In a promising movement, Sewell tried to feed Broome, but McCall cleverly intervened, and Kaile, on the Forest left, being unable to get the better of Chapman, ran the ball behind.

Forest had shown themselves a formidable force in the last 10 minutes, and after Ardron had seen a shot easily saved by Smith, Lawton gained possession, but his intended pass for Johnston failed to reach its mark and Whare duly cleared.

Following a throw-in on the right, Lawton lifted the ball into the goalmouth, and Walker intercepted the home centre's pass to Johnston to effect a grand clearance. A minute later Walker held a right foot drive from Evans.

It was a long time before Broome got into real action, and beating both McCall and Morley, he put the ball in front to Lawton, but when the centre-forward was about to shoot the ball ran away from him and Rawson cleared.

HALF-TIME:

NOTTS. COUNTY 0
NOTTM. FOREST 0

On resuming the Forest made tracks towards the Notts. goal and Morley was forced to place behind.

The County replied and Johnston, who had veered over to the right wing, beat both Whare and Anderson and then the ball ran behind.

A forward pass from Broome saw [illegible] between [illegible] and the

Record League crowd

The 46,000 all-ticket attendance for the match against Nottingham Forest on 22 April 1950 is the record home League crowd for Notts County.

Jackie Sewell heads the first goal in the Forest game. A 2-0 victory ensured that Notts were champions and promoted to Division 2.

(Above) Harry Adamson, goalkeeper Roy Smith and Norman Rigby (number 3) defending in the Forest match.

Lawton chases an opportunity ahead of Forest's Whare and Rawson.

The talented and popular Jackie Sewell was sold to Sheffield Wednesday in March 1951 for a new British record £34,000. Supporters were shocked and considered it a big mistake. Widespread protests were made in the press and to the directors. Above - Sewell and his colleagues are pictured saying their farewells.

A board meeting in 1949/50. (Below) Left to right: Walmsley (Treasurer), Barnes (Chairman), Cottee (President), Fisher (Secretary), Houghton (Manager), Linnell, Levy, Hubbard, Edwards. The same directors who had such bold plans for the club when they signed Lawton and others then threw the massive potential away. The sale of Sewell was the start of a policy which led to the long-term decline of Notts County. Cottee and Levy were part of a minority that opposed the decision and resigned after further policy differences in December 1951. In a statement they said the transfer was unnecessary and that *"we lost one of our best forwards at a time when we were trying to build up a formidable side"*. They later joined the ambitious Committee at Nottingham Forest and from then on nearly all the ambition was on the other side of the Trent. The seeds were sown - Forest would end the decade in the First Division, County in the Fourth. Where would Notts County be today if Cottee and Levey had won and Barnes and others had resigned instead?

Back to black & white stripes

Notts returned to black and white stripes for the start of season 1952/3. This is the team that played at Rotherham on 1 September 1952. Back (l to r): Bill Moore (Trainer), Billy Baxter, Harry Adamson, Tommy Deans, Gordon Bradley, Harry Jarvis, Tony Allen, Bill Evans. Front: Frank Broome, Jimmy Jackson, Cecil McCormack, Ron Wylie, Bob Crookes.

Action from the match at home to Blackburn Rovers on 13 December 1952. The 4 Notts players on the right are Harry Adamson, Tom Johnston, Tommy Deans (no. 2) and Billy Baxter. Although it went unnoticed it was Notts County's 2000th League game.

1954/5
The end of an era

The crowd on the Kop on 21 August 1954, part of the 29,528 attendance for the first match of the 1954/5 season against Derby County.

The team that played unchanged from the 3rd to the 6th round of the FA Cup in 1954/5. Back (l to r): Aubrey Southwell, Harry Adamson, Gordon Bradley, Leon Leuty, Bill Moore (Trainer). Front: Gordon Wills, Ron Wylie, Jimmy Jackson, Tommy Deans, 'Tot' Leverton, Albert Broadbent.

The 5th round FA Cup tie against Chelsea in 1954/5. Leon Leuty heads away in a crowded goalmouth, with Tommy Deans (no. 3) on the extreme right. The Magpies won 1-0.

Gordon Bradley and Leon Leuty defend against Chelsea's Roy Bentley in the 1954/5 cup-tie.

(Below) Notts reached the 6th round of the FA Cup for the first time since 1922. They played giant-killers York City, a Third Division (North) side who had already beaten 2 First Division teams. A crowd of 47,310, Notts' all-time record attendance, saw York win 1-0. Arthur Bottom is pictured scoring the goal that caused huge disappointment to Magpies' fans.

A training session in 1954/5. Left to right: Bill Moore (Trainer), George Poyser (Manager), Tommy Deans, Jack Taylor, Aubrey Southwell, Gordon Bradley, Harry Adamson, Leon Leuty, Ron Wylie and Tom Johnston.

An unfamiliar view from behind the Spion Kop goal taken by a supporter circa 1954. The goalkeeper is Gordon Bradley, Leon Leuty is in the centre and the other Notts player on the left is Tommy Deans.

The reserve side that made certain of the championship of the Midland League in 1954/5 with a 5-0 victory over Goole Town in the last match of the season (l to r):
Back: Vic Potts (Trainer), Frank Cruickshank, Pat Groome, Jimmy Linton, John McGrath, Ken Rawson, Bert Loxley. Front: Bill Coole, Don Roby, Bob Bulch, Gerry Carver, Bob Crookes.

9: To the Depths: 1955/6 to 1968/9

Main Events

1955/6 Death of club captain, Leon Leuty. Rapid break-up of successful 1954/5 side.

1957/8 Relegated to newly-constituted Division 3.

1958/9 Relegated to Division 4.

1959/60 Promoted to Division 3.

1962 Centenary celebrations.

1963/4 Relegated to Division 4.

1965/6 A financial crisis left the club close to extinction. Rescued by Bill Hopcroft.
Lowest-ever individual League match attendance at Meadow Lane.

1966/7 Missed having to apply for re-election by only a fraction.
Lowest average League attendance of the 20th century (until 'beaten' in 1996/7).

1968/9 Sank to the bottom of Division 4 on 21 September 1968 but later recovered to finish 19th.

Notable Players

Over 50 goals – Tony Hateley.

Over 200 appearances – Gerry Carver, Dick Edwards, Alex Gibson, Bert Loxley, Don Roby, John Sheridan, George Smith, Tony Hateley. (Hateley made the majority of his appearances in the 1960s but passed the 200 mark during his second spell with the club between 1970 and 1972)

Others – Jeff Astle, Dave Watson.

Leon Leuty died from leukaemia in December 1955. He was an outstanding player and a popular captain. His death shocked everyone connected with the club.

The Notts County and Leeds United teams line up in memory of Leon Leuty on 27 December 1955. The tragic event also symbolises the end of the post-war era in which many quality players had graced Meadow Lane.

Some had been foolishly sold in their prime and others had been retained into their 30s without adequate replacement. The entire defence and half-back line of the relatively successful 1954/5 team was over 30, one of the young forwards (Broadbent) was sold and the side soon broke up. Chairman Charles Barnes finally resigned in 1956 but the club's decline had already gone too far.

Tommy Lawton returned as manager in 1957 but relegation ensued. He was not given the money to strengthen the team and great players do not automatically make great managers. Next to Lawton is Ron Wylie and then, from right to left, Bert Loxley, Gordon Wills, Jimmy Jackson, Cyril Parry (partly hidden), Gordon Bradley, Don Roby, Peter Russell, Pat Groome and Frank Cruickshank.

Promotion 1959/60

The 1959/60 team that was promoted from Division 4. Standing (l to r): Alex Gibson, John Butler, Bob Forrest, George Smith, Bert Loxley, Tony Hateley, Harry Noon. Sitting: Jack Wheeler (Trainer), Don Roby, Chris Joyce, John Sheridan, Gerry Carver, Peter Bircumshaw, Frank Hill (Manager). On ground: Alan Withers, Stan Newsham, Roy Horobin.

George Smith, Alex Gibson and Bert Loxley in action in the last home match of the 1959/60 promotion season against Darlington. Notts still needed the points to make sure of promotion and a 5-4 victory was enough to start the celebrations.

Tony Hateley challenges for a high cross in the 1959/60 game at home Darlington. Bob Forrest is on the right.

NOTTS. COUNTY
FOOTBALL CLUB
SEASON 1959/60

The Oldest Established
Football Club
in the Country

Players Promotion
Souvenir Handbook

PRICE TWO SHILLINGS

The1960 promotion handbook.

Bob Forrest, captain of the 1959/60 promotion side.

The Notts County staff in the 1961/2 centenary year. Back (l to r): Peter Bircumshaw, Jeff Astle, John Butler, Dick Edwards, Tony Bircumshaw. Standing: Gerry Carver, Alex Gibson, George Smith, Bert Loxley, Peter Butler, John Sheridan, Brian Moore. Sitting: Jack Wheeler (Trainer), Chris Joyce, Roy Horobin, Bob Forrest, Tony Hateley, Frank Hill (Manager). On ground: Harry Noon, Alan Withers.

100

As the first professional club in the country to celebrate their centenary, on 2 May 1962 Notts played an England eleven that was preparing for the 1962 World Cup. Hateley and Gibson gave inspired displays but England won 3-1.

CENTENARY MATCH

World Cup man Peacock plays second fiddle to Alex Gibson

By Tony Pritchett

NOTTS. COUNTY .... 1 FA XI 3

MORE than 11,000 fans—nearly three times as many as saw County's last Third Division game and much better than the season's average—filed into historic Meadow-lane last night to see an international-studded FA side meet County in the long-awaited match to celebrate the club's centenary.

The star-packed representativ side, containing four members o England's World Cup party, wer the undoubted attraction, but I fanc that most of those 11,000 wer hoping that the Magpies coul somehow put it across their dis tinguished opposition.

It soon became obvious that tha would not happen; but at least th Meadow-lane faithfuls had a inspired display by Tony Hateley t cheer them.

The tall Notts. leader shrugged off the indifferent form which has haunted him lately, to turn in a sparkling display at a time when it could do him most good—in front of the directors and managers from many of the 92 Football League clubs.

Hateley, playing the game as if it were a Cup Final, instead of a casual friendly, made the display of Alan Peacock, England's surprise choice to go on the Chile trip, a big disappointment.

Splendid goal

While Hateley chased everything and won the biggest roar of the night

In the centenary match, Hateley is beaten to a cross by Hodgkinson, the England goalkeeper.

(Above) White shirts made a comeback for one season in 1962/3. George Smith collects the ball in the Barnsley match on 1 September 1962. Alex Gibson and Bert Loxley in the background are the other Notts players.

Back to white shirts

(Right) Gerry Carver leads the team out for the game against QPR on 23 February 1962. He is followed by Smith, Gibson, Tony Bircumshaw, Sheridan and Edwards.

Personal Recollections: Colin Slater
The Save of the Sixties

The unthinkable first real threat to Notts County's existence happened late in 1965 – but, in football as in life, the unthinkable can and does happen.

In November, 1961 the five-man board of directors made a decision based rather more on personality clashes than football judgment when not renewing the contract of their manager, Frank Hill who had been appointed in October 1958 and had masterminded the club's promotion to Division Three in 1960. Having consolidated their position in 1960-61, he then went 17 League matches into the 1961-62 campaign. It was a decision the board should have come to regret.

The apparent beneficiary was Tim Coleman, who had been a player at Arsenal in the Thirties, as had Hill. A Nottinghamshire man, he was working at Meadow Lane as a coach when offered the vacancy. Given the subsequent turn of events he was more of a victim.

Len Machin had been chairman since 1957 and is forever remembered for his pledge to make Notts "*the Arsenal of the Midlands*". He suddenly announced that a new manager would succeed Coleman, who would revert to his former role. Eddie Lowe, a former England midfield player with Aston Villa and Fulham, would take his first (and, as it transpired, last) managerial position as from 1 July 1963. The players' response was immediate: Twenty-four hours after the announcement they routed Colchester United 6-0 and, before the end of the season, lifted the Nottinghamshire County Cup by beating Mansfield Town and Forest. These were very clear intimations of dressing room support for Coleman.

The annual meeting of shareholders, held in mid-July, gave no hint of the looming crisis. A profit of £23,400 was reported, cutting the overall deficit to around £25,000.

A day later Lowe made his first signing – outside left Mike Barber from Queen's Park Rangers for around £12,000. But before the month was out there came a pivotal moment when the board agreed to sell highly-rated young centre-forward Tony Hateley to Aston Villa for £25,000. On the evening the transfer was completed - 29 July, 1963 - Hill, now manager of Charlton Athletic, telephoned local journalist Colin Slater: *"Doesn't Eddie appreciate that Hateley is the one player who will keep him in work?"* he asked.

Lowe's first season, 1963-64, began badly, deteriorated further - and Notts were relegated, back to the Fourth Division. They were to spend seven wasted years there, with a consequent effect on income through greatly reduced attendances, less support for commercial activities - and, vitally, losing ground to Forest, who were more successful and better supported. However, events off the field proved more crucial. In February, 1964 the board was shocked to be informed by Machin, who ran a knitwear firm at Gotham, that he had withdrawn his money from the club - estimated at £25,000 - save for £5. He apparently explained to his fellow-directors that he had not obtained their prior approval because, when funds had previously been needed to pay wages or meet other demands, he had been expected to come to the rescue without consulting the board.

In conversations with me he appeared confident of his position, partly, it was thought, because he believed he would continue to have the support of two other directors, Peter Machin (his son) and Ernest Hodson, even if Fred Williamson and Stanley Thomas opposed him. However, attitudes had apparently been changed by Machin's withdrawal of his money. When the board met on 2 March, 1964 a vote of no confidence in him was carried with Hodson joining Williamson and Thomas to form a majority.

Machin was out of the chair after seven years and Williamson was installed. Two months later, at a meeting of shareholders, Machin was voted off the board, which was reconstituted. Lou Levin, Harry Moss, Bill Laurie and Albert Pounder joined. They were followed by Bernard Bateman representing the new Notts County Association, a brainchild of Levin's for vital fund-raising purposes and the first instance of supporters having a representative on the board.

Without the support of Machin, who had appointed him and always championed him, Lowe was less secure and was sacked in April, 1965 - with the ever-loyal Coleman reappointed. Under him Notts lost only three of 15 League matches at the start of 1965-66 but the financial position was worsening and a first round FA Cup defeat at Southend was a heavy blow, with Notts looking forlornly for the extra revenue that a good Cup run brings.

The board was called to a crisis session. The date was Sunday 5 December, 1965 and the venue was Williamson's home. During the evening he telephoned and asked me to join them. I walked into an atmosphere that resembled a gathering of mourners. Having expected to be advised of steps to stabilise the finances I was instead told that they and Notts had come to the end of the road and there was no way of keeping the club going - and therefore no hope. because he lacked confidence in the management I asked whether they were *absolutely* sure nothing could be done. Only one man, they said, seemed willing to come forward.

He was not connected with Notts in any way - not even a season ticket holder - and he was backing off . I argued that, given those circumstances, something surely had to be done to give him the necessary confidence. Yes - but what? I suggested that I should be allowed to approach Andy Beattie, a distinguished figure in the game and, ironically, a neighbour of Williamson's. He was a former manager of Forest and of several other clubs. I knew him well and had a high opinion of his abilities and - not least - his integrity. At nearly midnight it was agreed.

I met Beattie the following morning, outlining the extremely grave position to him. His considered response was to offer to work at Notts as an *unpaid* adviser and to approach his great friend Peter Doherty to see if he was willing to join him. Beattie was Scotland's first national team manager while Doherty held a similar position with Northern Ireland. He was now living between Bristol and Weston-super-Mare and was telephoned. He agreed to help on the same terms. Events moved so swiftly than on Friday 10 December the *Nottingham Evening Post* led its front page with the news of the joint appointment of Beattie and Doherty. I think I was entitled to my scoop!

Within days director Harry Moss and I were visiting the benefactor, Bill Hopcroft. We went to his business in Carlton Hill where he ran motor car auctions and, in his office, he handed over his cheque for £10,000. That is what it cost, in the values of those days, for Hopcroft to be the saviour of Notts County. He briefly became chairman, succeeding Williamson and then giving way to Jack Dunnett, whom he served for a while as vice-chairman.

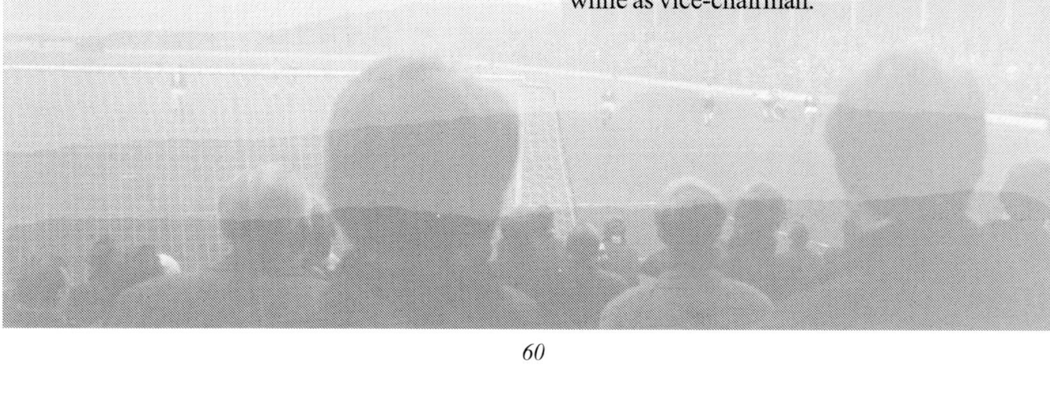

The fight for survival

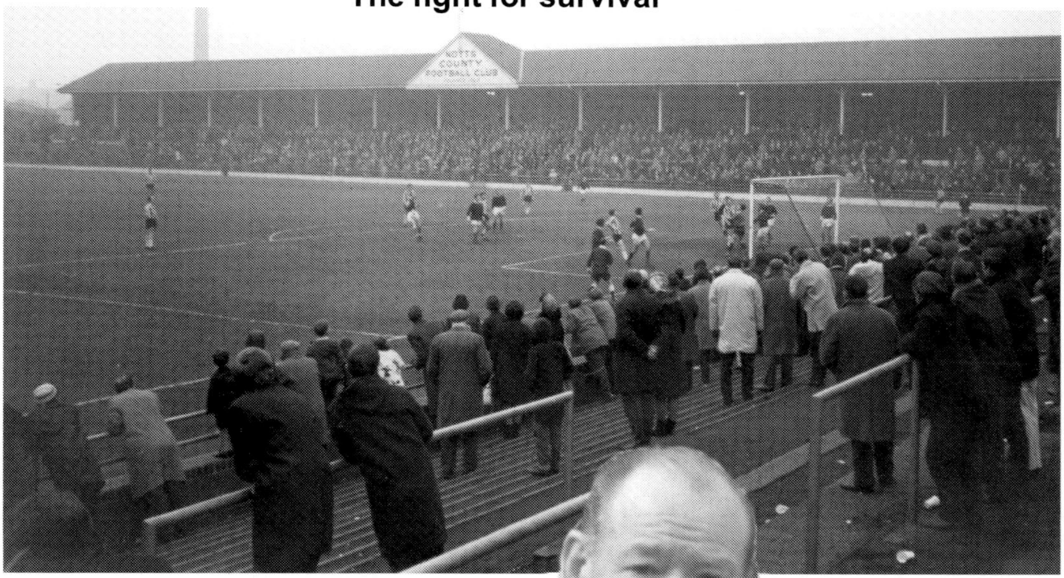

A sparse crowd in the mid-1960s. The club had been so badly directed since the early 1950s that in 1966/7 the average League crowd was down to 4,354, the lowest of the 20th century (until 1996/7 when the figure was 4,239). On 2 April 1966 only 1,927 turned up at Meadow Lane to see County play the League match against Chesterfield.

Bill Hopcroft put £10,000 into Notts County in 1966 and saved them from going out of business.

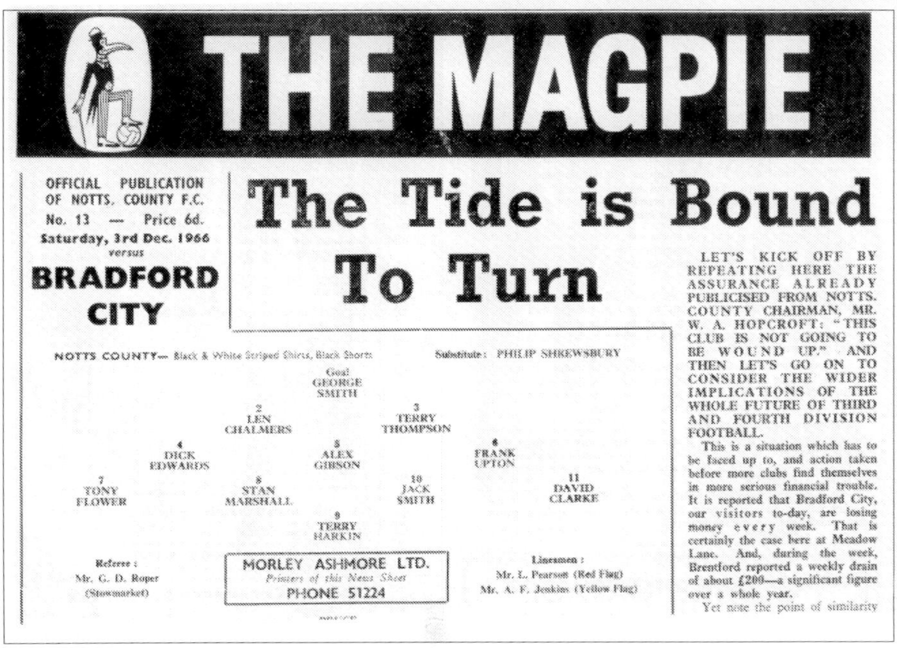

THE MAGPIE

OFFICIAL PUBLICATION OF NOTTS. COUNTY F.C.
No. 13 — Price 6d.
Saturday, 3rd Dec. 1966
versus
BRADFORD CITY

The Tide is Bound To Turn

NOTTS COUNTY— Black & White Striped Shirts, Black Shorts
Substitute: PHILIP SHREWSBURY

Goal GEORGE SMITH
2 LEN CHALMERS
3 TERRY THOMPSON
4 DICK EDWARDS
5 ALEX GIBSON
6 FRANK UPTON
7 TONY FLOWER
8 STAN MARSHALL
9 TERRY HARKIN
10 JACK SMITH
11 DAVID CLARKE

Referee: Mr. G. D. Roper (Stowmarket)

MORLEY ASHMORE LTD.
Printers of this News Sheet
PHONE 51224

Linesmen: Mr. L. Pearson (Red Flag) Mr. A. F. Jenkins (Yellow Flag)

LET'S KICK OFF BY REPEATING HERE THE ASSURANCE ALREADY PUBLICISED FROM NOTTS. COUNTY CHAIRMAN, MR. W. A. HOPCROFT: "THIS CLUB IS NOT GOING TO BE WOUND UP." AND THEN LET'S GO ON TO CONSIDER THE WIDER IMPLICATIONS OF THE WHOLE FUTURE OF THIRD AND FOURTH DIVISION FOOTBALL.

This is a situation which has to be faced up to, and action taken before more clubs find themselves in more serious financial trouble. It is reported that Bradford City, our visitors to-day, are losing money every week. That is certainly the case here at Meadow Lane. And, during the week, Brentford reported a weekly drain of about £200—a significant figure over a whole year.

Yet note the point of similarity

The financial crisis was front page news in this programme from December 1966.

11: Back Up Again: The 1970s

Main Events

1969/70	Recovery started under manager Jimmy Sirrel and chairman Jack Dunnett.
1970/1	Promoted to Division 3. Champions of Division 4.
1972/3	Promoted to Division 2. Reached round 5 of League Cup.
1975/6	5th in Division 2 - best League position since 1928/9. Reached round 5 of League Cup.

Notable Players

Over 50 goals – Les Bradd, Don Masson, Mick Vinter.

Over 200 appearances – Les Bradd, Bill Brindley, Steve Carter, Arthur Mann, Don Masson, Eric McManus, David Needham, Ray O'Brien, Pedro Richards, Brian Stubbs, Bob Worthington.

International – Ray O'Brien (Irish Republic).

The transformation of Notts County

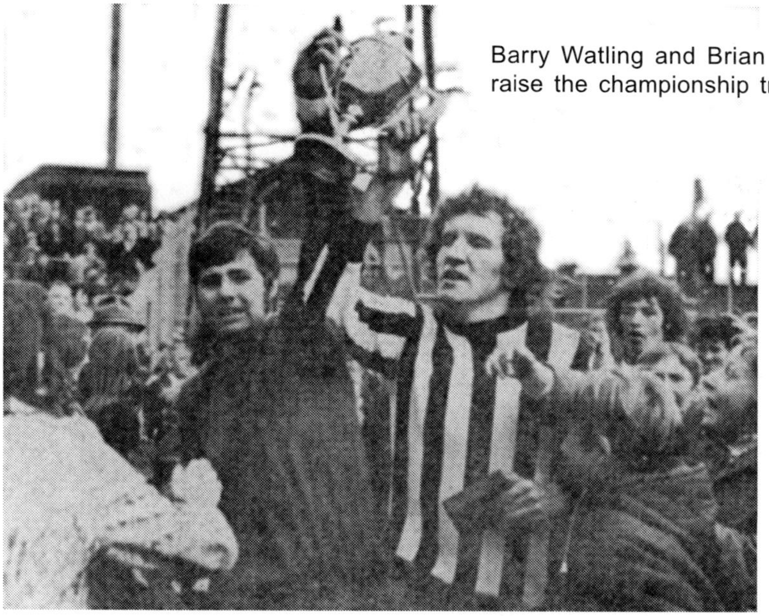
Barry Watling and Brian Stubbs raise the championship trophy

Celebrations in the dressing room

Promotion 1970/1

(Opposite page - middle)
After hitting the bottom of the Fourth Division in 1968, the Magpies would rise to the top of the First Division (very briefly) in 1983. They were promoted 3 times in 10 years with Don Masson as captain, Jack Dunnett as chairman, Jimmy Sirrel as manager and Jack Wheeler as trainer, on each occasion. The transformation began when Dunnett became chairman in 1969 and Jimmy Sirrel was appointed manager in November of the same year.

(Opposite page bottom)
The team that won the Division 4 championship in 1970/1. Back (l to r): Mick Jones, David Needham, Les Bradd, Barry Watling, Brian Stubbs, Bob Worthington, Jack Wheeler (Trainer). Front: Jon Nixon, Richie Barker, Don Masson, Jimmy Sirrel (Manager), Tony Hateley, Bill Brindley, Charlie Crickmore.

Programme for the last game of the successful 1970/1 season. At the end Don Masson and the team parade the Division 4 championship trophy surrounded by jubilant supporters after the game.

Tony Hateley returned to Meadow Lane on 7 November 1970 after an absence of more than 7 years in which he played for several First Division clubs including Chelsea and Liverpool. He was famous for his powerful heading ability and in his 2 periods with Notts he scored 129 League and Cup goals in 272 games.

Promotion 1972/3

Manager Jimmy Sirrel is applauded by the fans after he has steered Notts to promotion for the second time in 3 seasons.

The players celebrate in the dressing room after Notts have made sure of promotion by beating Tranmere on the last day of the 1972/3 season.

The players surrounded by happy supporters

David Needham and Les Bradd open the champagne.

Don Masson's excellence in midfield played a major part in 3 promotions as Notts rose from the Fourth Division to the First between 1971 and 1981. He was sold to QPR in 1974 because County needed the money but returned via Derby County in 1978. In total he played 440 League and Cup games and scored 96 goals.

All the leading members of the 1972/3 promotion side are pictured in this team group taken before the start of the following season. Eddie Cliff and Eric Probert were new signings for 1973/4. Back (l to r): Eddie Cliff, Kevin Randall, David Needham, Eric McManus, Roy Brown, Bob Worthington, Brian Stubbs, Les Bradd. Front: Jon Nixon, Bill Brindley, Arthur Mann, Steve Carter, Don Masson, Willie Carlin, Eric Probert.

The mid-1970s

In 1972/3 the Magpies got through to round 5 of the League Cup. Here Les Bradd is pictured scoring a brilliant goal against Stoke in round 4.

In 1975/6 Notts again reached round 5 of the League Cup. Ian Scanlon heads the winner as the Magpies beat Leeds 1-0 at Elland Road in round 3 on 8 October 1975.

(Below) Les Bradd and Leeds' Billy Bremner feature in the action as Notts attack the Leeds goal at Elland Road in the 1975/6 League Cup match.

Arthur Mann in action at Everton in round 4 of the League Cup in 1975/6, with Brian Stubbs in the background. As the scoreboard shows it was a 2-2 draw and Notts won the replay 2-0.

Coincidentally the Magpies met Leeds again in 1975/6, at Meadow Lane in round 3 of the FA Cup. This time Leeds won 1-0. Ray O'Brien faces Leeds' Paul Madeley (no. 5) as Billy Bremner races in on the left.

In the same cup-tie, Les Bradd outjumps Leeds' Norman Hunter and David Harvey, with Paul Madeley on the right.

Brian Stubbs is presented with the Shipp Cup, a minor competition played before the start of the 1975/6 season. Left to right: Ray O'Brien, Stubbs, David McVay, David Needham, Eric McManus.

The 1976/7 team. Back (l to r): Ian Scanlon, Mick Vinter, Brian Stubbs, Les Bradd. Middle: Jack Wheeler (Trainer), David McVay, Eric McManus, Pedro Richards, Frank Lane, Ian Bolton, Colin Addison (Coach), Ron Fenton (Manager). Front: Dave Smith, Steve Carter, David Needham, Arthur Mann, Roy O'Brien.

The demolition in 1978 of the Meadow Lane stand which had been there since the stadium was built in 1910.

Striker Les Bradd in action for Notts against Sunderland on 3 April 1976. Les is the club's record goalscorer with 125 League goals and a further 11 in the major Cup competitions. He was signed from Rotherham in1967 and made 433 League and Cup appearances before moving to Stockport in 1978.

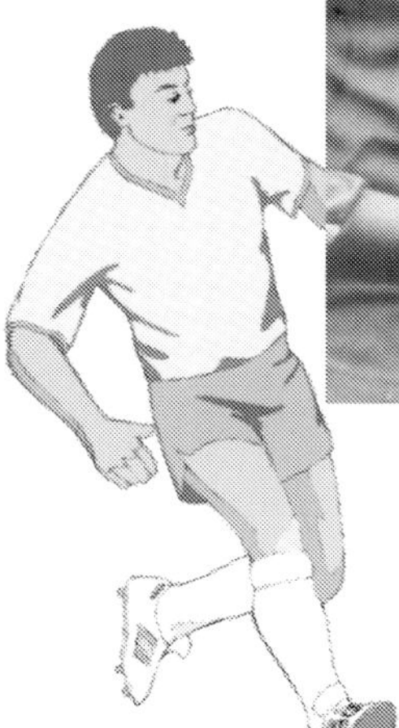

Two earlier Notts County record goalscorers, Jackie Sewell (centre) and Tony Hateley (right), make a presentation to Les Bradd when he became the club's all-time record scorer in 1976.

12: Up and Down: The 1980s

Main Events

1980/1 Promoted to Division 1.

1981/2 Finished 15th in Division 1 – the best League position since 1924/5.

1982/3 15th again in Division 1.

1983/4 Relegated to Division 2. Reached round 6 of FA Cup.

1984/5 Relegated to Division 3.

1987 Derek Pavis took over the club.

1987/8 Made the play-offs but failed to win promotion.

Notable Players

Over 50 goals – Trevor Christie, Iain McCulloch, Ian McParland.

Over 200 appearances – Tristan Benjamin, Mark Goodwin, David Hunt, Mick Leonard, Iain McCulloch, Ian McParland.

Internationals – Martin O'Neill (Northern Ireland), Jim McDonagh (Irish Republic), Rachid Harkouk (Algeria), John Chiedozie (Nigeria), Aki Lahtinen (Finland).

Promotion 1980/1

The 1980/1 promotion side. Back (l to r): Trevor Christie, Eddie Kelly, Mick Leonard, Raddy Avramovic, Pedro Richards, Rachid Harkouk. Middle: Jack Wheeler (Trainer), David Hunt, Gary Wood, Brian Kilcline, Brian Stubbs, Ray O'Brien, Tristan Benjamin, Mick Walker (Youth Coach). Front: Don Masson, Paul Hooks, Gordon Mair, Jimmy Sirrel (Manager), Howard Wilkinson (Coach), Paul Manns, Iain McCulloch, Jim Doherty.

Rachid Harkouk scores the second goal in the 2-0 win at Chelsea that took Notts back into the First Division on 2 May 1981.

Iain McCulloch scores against Cambridge in the last game of the 1980/1 season as Notts say farewell to Division 2.

Jimmy Sirrel and the players receive the joyful congratulations of supporters after the Cambridge match. Sirrell guided Notts from the Fourth to the First Division in 10 years.

The First Division years

On 29 August 1981 the Magpies played their first match in Division 1 for 55 years. Iain McCulloch scores the only goal as Notts win away at reigning League Champions, Aston Villa.

The 1982/3 First Division side.

Back (l to r): Pedro Richards, Trevor Christie, Mick Leonard, Raddy Avramovic, David Hunt, Tristan Benjamin, Ray O'Brien.

Middle: Jack Wheeler (Physio), Paul Hooks, Nigel Worth-ington, Aki Lahtinen, Brian Kilcline, Rachid Harkouk, Gary Wood, Mick Walker (Youth Coach), Howard Wilkinson (Team Manager).

Front: Iain McCulloch, Paul Manns, Gordon Mair, Jimmy Sirrel (Club Manager), Ian Mc-Parland, John Chied-ozie, Mark Goodwin.

The Villa Park scoreboard tells the story of Notts' unexpected but welcome success.

Action from the Manchester United match at Meadow Lane in 1981/2. The Notts players, left to right, are Harkouk, Kilcline and Benjamin. The United players are Ray Wilkins (left) and Gary Birtles.

With minutes left on the clock, and Notts a goal down, David Hunt scores a late equaliser at home to Arsenal in 1981/2........

....Then with seconds left, Brian Kilcline scores the winner.

Trevor Cristie scores from the penalty spot against Chelsea in round 3 of the Milk Cup on 9 November 1982. Notts won 2-0 but went out to West Ham in the next round.

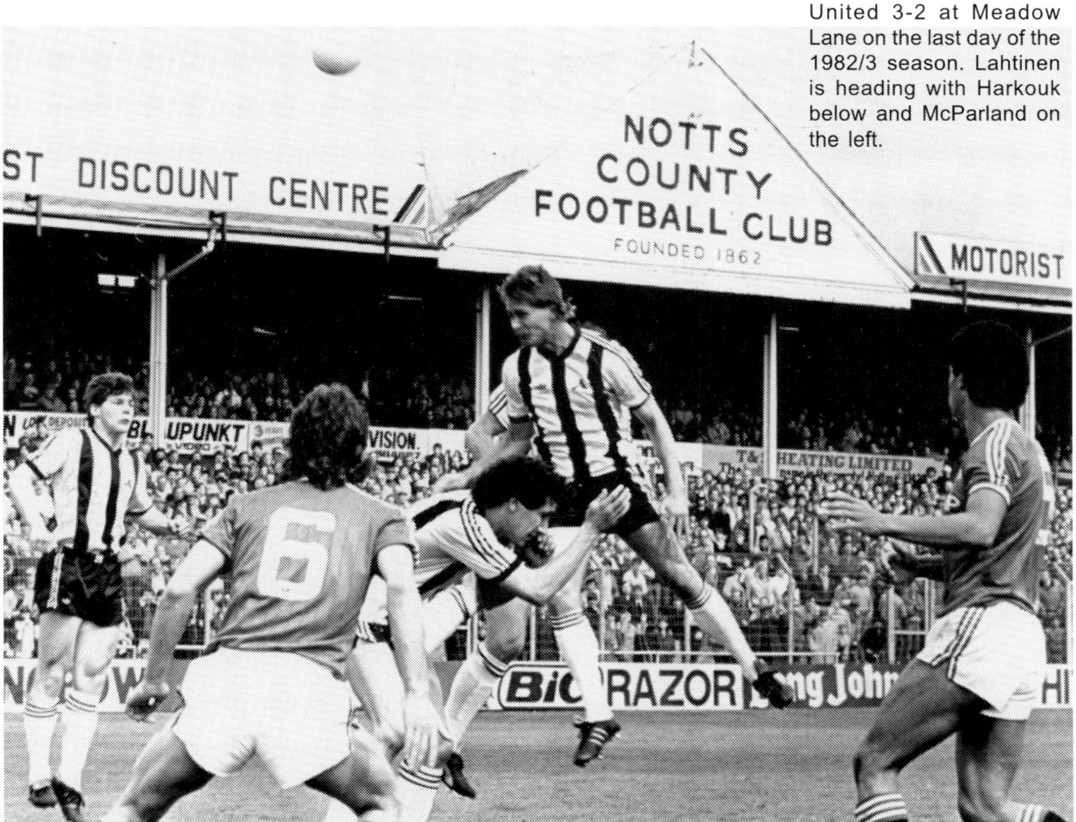

Notts beat Manchester United 3-2 at Meadow Lane on the last day of the 1982/3 season. Lahtinen is heading with Harkouk below and McParland on the left.

(Right)
John Chiedozie scores the goal that beat Middlesbrough after a brilliant solo run in the 5th round of the FA Cup on 18 February 1984.

(Below)
John Chiedozie scores against Everton in round 6 of the FA Cup on 10 March 1984 but Notts lost 2-1.

12: Personal Recollections – Colin Slater
Dunnett Gets a 'Lifeline'

It was well over 30 years (from that dire situation in 1965), when Notts were next in danger of being wound up, though a shadow was cast over the club in August, 1986. Jack Dunnett reported an overall deficit of £1.8m, intimated his intention to retire at the end of the season and said there needed to be *a 'Blueprint for Survival.'*

This included the introduction of the Lifeline fund-raising scheme – an immediate hit and operating still. The old Sherwood Rooms (scene of the banquet in 1962 to mark the club's Centenary), by now renamed the Astoria, was the venue on Monday 15 September.

Fans responded magnificently with 1,500 packed inside and 300 unable to gain admission. Dunnett had invited me to front an emotional evening. All the players were there and the biggest cheers were reserved for two icons - Sirrel and Lawton.

A few people have since tried to claim Lifeline as their brainchild. The credit for it belongs only to one man - Alf Davies, who had pioneered the scheme as commercial manager of Bolton Wanderers. A few years later he became chief executive at Headingley when I was marketing manager at Trent Bridge and we not only renewed our friendship but worked closely together - this time for the good of cricket. Small world!

The new Notts 1987/8

A new era began when Derek Pavis took over Notts County in the summer of 1987. The new board of directors was (l to r): Derek Pavis, Frank Allcock, Bill Hopcroft and John Mounteney.

The team group at the start of 1987/8 included many new signings. Back (l to r): David Thompson, Paul Smalley, Darren Davis, Dean Yates, Gary Mills, Ian McParland. Middle: Gary Lund, Dale Belford, Gary Birtles, Paul Hart, Andy Gray, Mick Leonard, Craig Jackson. Front: Eddie Snook, David Kevan, Sean Kimberley, John Barnwell (Manager), Geoff Pike, Paul Barnes, Mark Harbottle.

Sunderland had dropped into the Third Division for the only time in their history and went straight back up as champions in 1987/8. They came to Meadow Lane on 31 October and Notts beat them 2-1 with 2 goals from Gary Birtles. Here Birtles (left) scores the winner, watched by Ian McParland (centre) and Geoff Pike.

The Magpies made the play-offs in 1987/8. Dejected Paul Barnes (left) and Gary Lund leave the pitch after Notts have lost the semi-final first leg 3-1 at home to Walsall on 15 May. County drew the second leg 1-1 and so stayed in Division 3.

14: Up and Down Again: The 1990s

Main Events

1989/90	Promoted to Division 2 after play-off at Wembley.
1990/1	Promoted to Division 1 after play-off at Wembley. Reached round 6 of FA Cup.
1991/2	Relegated. (Division 2 was renamed Division 1 on the formation of the Premiership).
1992	New stands erected on three sides of Meadow Lane.
1993/4	Defeated in the Anglo-Italian Cup final at Wembley.
1994	Stadium rebuilding completed with the erection of the new main stand, the Derek Pavis stand.
1994/5	Relegated to Division 2. Won the Anglo-Italian Cup at Wembley.
1995/6	Reached play-off final at Wembley but failed to win promotion.
1996/7	Relegated to Division 3 (the old Fourth Division). The average home League crowd of 4,239 was the lowest of the 20th century.
1997/8	Promoted to Division 2. Champions of Division 3 in a record-breaking season.

Notable Players

Over 50 goals – Gary Lund, Tommy Johnson.
Over 200 appearances – Steve Cherry, Mark Draper, Gary Lund, Charlie Palmer, Phil Turner, Dean Yates, Darren Ward.
Internationals – Kevin Wilson (Northern Ireland), Darren Ward (Wales).
Other – Steve Finnan

Promotion 1989/90

The 1989/90 promotion squad. Back (l to r): Geoff Pike, David Norton, Willie McStay, Wayne Fairclough, Scott Machin, Paul Cox, David Kevan. Middle: Phil Robinson, Charlie Palmer, Nicky Law, Dean Yates, Steve Cherry, Aidan Davison, Craig Short, Don O'Riordan, Phil Stant, John Newman (Asst. Manager). Front: Gary Lund, Paul Barnes, Tommy Johnson, Neil Warnock (Manager), Phil Turner, Mark Draper, Nicky Platnauer.

(Top)
Manager Neil Warnock leads the team out for the Division 3 play-off final at Wembley on 27 May 1990 against Tranmere Rovers. It was Notts County's first-ever appearance at Wembley.

(Above))
Dean Yates threatens the Tranmere goal.

(Left)
Craig Short has scored Notts' second goal.

The players on hearing the final whistle. Notts have won 2-0.

The jubilant Wembley team group. Back (l to r): Platnauer, Turner, Norton, Palmer, Bartlett, Robinson, Yates, Cherry. Front: Draper, O'Riordan, Lund, Thomas, Johnson, Craig Short (no. 4).

The FA Cup run of 1990/91

Gary Lund taps in a late winner in the FA Cup 5th round at home to Manchester City on 16 February 1991.

Mark Draper leaves behind Tottenham's Nayim and Paul Gascoigne in the FA Cup 6th round tie at White Hart Lane on 10 March. The Magpies put up a gallant fight but lost 2-1.

Promotion 1990/91

The 1990/1 promotion squad (below). Back (l to r): Craig Finch, Shaun Browne, Paul Cox, Don O'Riordan, Richard Walker, Mark Telford, Anthony Thompson, Stephen Aldridge, Mark Wells. Middle: Mick Jones (Asst. Manager), Phil Stant, Charlie Palmer, Dean Yates, Steve Cherry, Kevin Blackwell, Craig Short, Gary Lund, Nicky Platnauer, David Wilson (Physio). Front: Phil Robinson, David Norton, Tommy Johnson, Phil Turner, Derek Pavis (Chairman), Neil Warnock (Manager), Mark Draper, Kevin Bartlett, Dean Thomas, Gary Chapman.

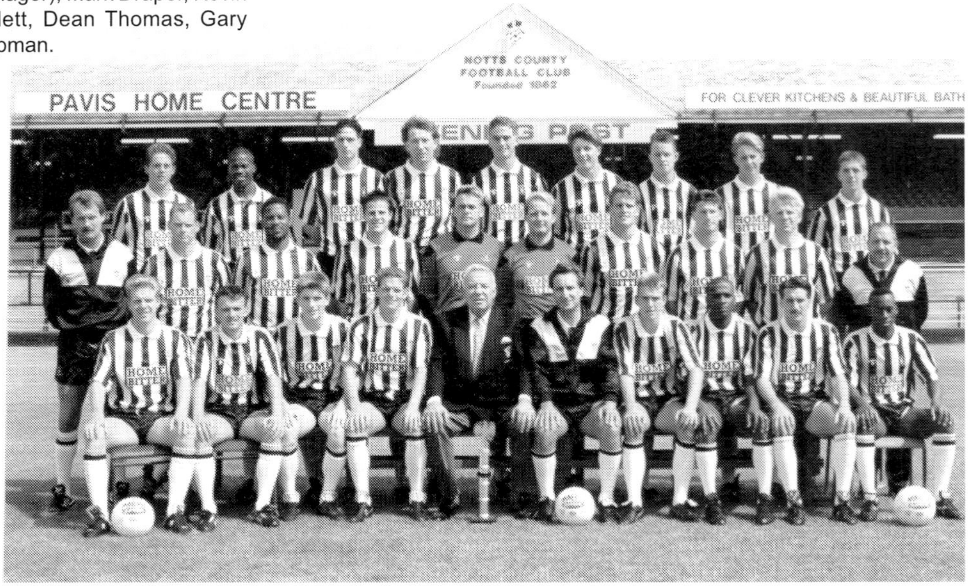

The Notts and Brighton teams take the field at Wembley for the Division 2 play-off final on 2 June 1991.

Tommy Johnson scores one of his 2 goals in a 3-1 victory for the Magpies.

The trophy presentation. Left to right: Phil Turner, Dean Yates, Tommy Johnson, Kevin Bartlett.

Tommy Johnson and Neil Warnock.

The Wembley team group. Back (l to r): Neil Warnock, Craig Short, Steve Cherry, Chris Short, Dave Regis, Paul Harding, Alan Paris, Kevin Bartlett, Mick Jones (Asst. Manager). Front: David Wilson (Physio), Don O'Riordan, Kevin Bartlett, Dean Yates, Phil Turner, Tommy Johnson, Mark Draper, Dean Thomas.

Back in the dressing room.

One of 3 new stands erected in the summer of 1992, the County Road stand was later dedicated to former manager Jimmy Sirrel.

The new Kop stand is used for the first time on 22 August 1992 when Leicester City are the visitors.

The rebuilding of the Meadow Lane stadium

In 1994 the ground changes were completed with the construction of a new main stand, known as the Derek Pavis Stand.

The new Meadow Lane end or Family stand in use for the first time on 22 August 1992.

Charlie Palmer has just scored the famous winner against Nottingham Forest at Meadow Lane on 12 February 1994. Paul Devlin is on the right.

Kevin Wilson is Notts County's most capped player with 15 appearances for Northern Ireland during his time with the club between 1992 and 1994.

Wembley 1994

Manager Mick Walker leads the team out for the Anglo-Italian Cup final against Brescia at Wembley on 20 March 1994.

Gary McSwegan in action at Wembley.

(Below) Notts have lost 1-0 to Brescia and the disappointment shows as the defeated players file off at the end.

Wembley 1995

Notts are back at Wembley for another Anglo-Italian Cup final on 19 March 1995,
this time against Ascoli. Devon White heads the winner in a 2-1 victory.

The Anglo-Italian Cup winners of 1995 with the trophy: Back (l to r): Mick Galloway, Michael Emenalo,
Dennis Pettitt (Physio), Steve Cherry, Shaun Murphy, Devon White, Tony Agana, Chris Short, Paul Reece.
Front: Tommy Gallagher, Michael Simpson, Phil Turner, Michael Johnson,
Gary Mills (leaning forward), Paul Devlin, Andy Legg.

Promotion 1997/8

The record-breaking Division 3 champions of 1997/8. Back (l to r): Justin Jackson, Alex Dyer, Matt Redmile, Darren Ward, Gary Jones, Dennis Pearce, Shaun Cunnington. Middle: Roger Cleary (Physio), Andy Hughes, Sean Farrell, Gary Strodder, Ian Richardson, Steve Finnan, Phil Robinson, Alan Young (Youth Team Coach). Front: Craig Dudley, Ian Hendon, Sam Allardyce (Manager), Derek Pavis (Chairman), Mark Smith (Assistant Manager), Paul Mitchell, Mark Robson.

Notts County's 4000th League match is highlighted in the first home programme after the event. The landmark game itself was away at Rochdale on 10 January 1998. The 3000th game had been at home to Nottingham Forest in 1974/5, the 2000th at home to Blackburn in 1952/3 and the 1000th away to West Ham in 1921/2.

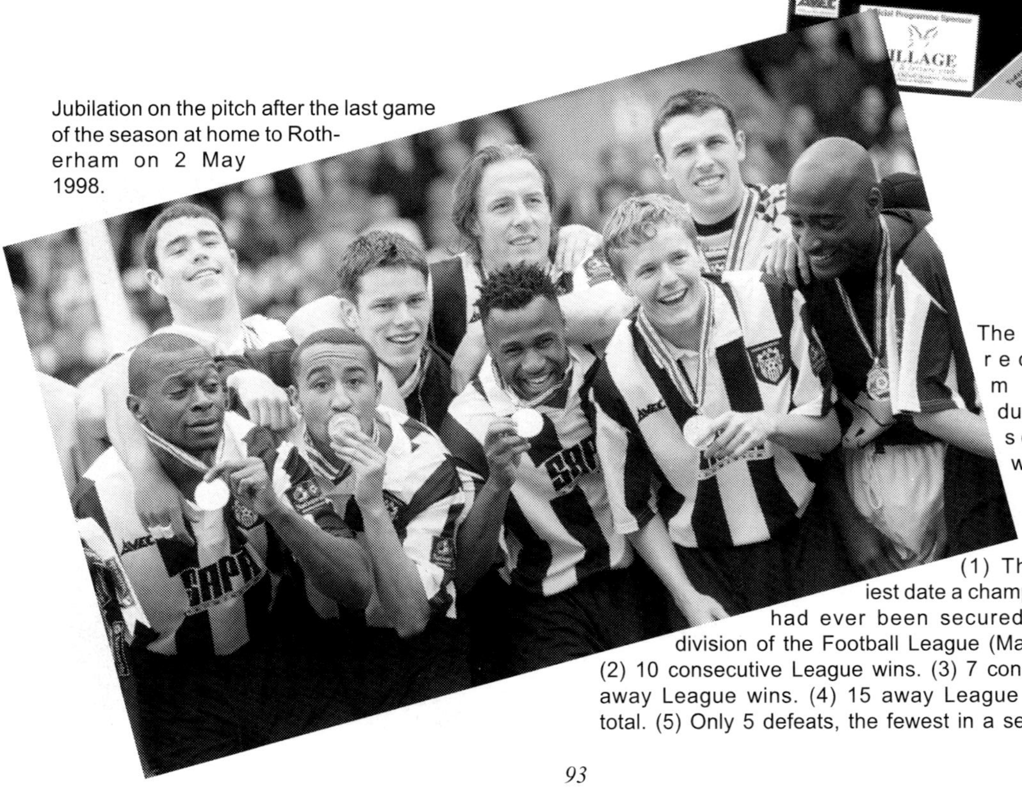

Jubilation on the pitch after the last game of the season at home to Rotherham on 2 May 1998.

The all-time records made during the season were:

(1) The earliest date a championship had ever been secured in any division of the Football League (March 28). (2) 10 consecutive League wins. (3) 7 consecutive away League wins. (4) 15 away League wins in total. (5) Only 5 defeats, the fewest in a season.

15: Fight For Survival: 2000/1 to 2003/4

Main Events

Off the pitch

2000 Start of a proposed takeover of the club from Derek Pavis in September 2000.

2002 Funding for completion of the takeover was withdrawn in February 2002. A cash crisis forced the club into administration on 17 June 2002.

2003 Events unfolded with many twists and turns and the club came close to liquidation and expulsion from the League. Notts County finally came out of administration on 3 December 2003, when funds raised by newly-formed groups, the Blenheim Consortium and the Supporters' Trust,enabled them to take over the club. One supporter put £3 million into the club.

On the pitch

2001/2 The 'Great Escape'. Notts avoided relegation with a last day win following a late run of good results.

2003/4 Relegated. (For the start of 2004/5 Division 3 was renamed League 2, i.e. the lowest level of League football).

Notable Players

Over 50 goals – Danny Allsopp, Mark Stallard.

Over 200 appearances – Ian Baraclough, Ian Richardson, Mark Stallard.

In 2001/2 Notts looked down and out after just 6 wins all season up to early March. Then came an amazing turnaround in March and April as 7 of the last 10 games were won. This period was dubbed the 'Great Escape' as the unthinkable avoidance of relegation seemed increasingly possible.

The Great Escape was finally achieved in the last game of the season, at home to Huddersfield. Danny Allsopp celebrates after scoring in Notts 2-1 victory in front of a big crowd of 15,618.

Manager Billy Dearden receives the appreciation of the crowd.

(Above) **Danny Allsopp's** 11 goals were a major factor in Notts' success in the Great Escape. In all he scored 25 League and Cup goals in 2001/2 and won the Player of the Year award. His career record was 51 goals in 119 games from 1999 to 2003.

(Above) **Ian Richardson's** commitment and inspired displays in defence have made him a favourite with the fans. He won the Player of the Year award in 2003/4 and was joint-winner in 1998/9. Between 1996 and the end of 2003/4 he had made 287 League and Cup appearances.

(Right) **Ian Baraclough** had 2 spells with Notts, first as a left-back and later as a midfielder. He played 242 games in the periods 1995-98 and 2001-04.

Mark Stallard was a popular striker who won the Player of the Year award in 2000/1 and 2002/3.

He was signed from Wycombe in 1999 and his transfer to Barnsley in 2004 reduced the wage bill. He scored 77 League and Cup goals in 209 appearances.

Administration

300 supporters attended a meeting on 14 January 2003 to set up a Supporters Trust to help the club in its financial crisis. The gathering is addressed by a representative of Supporters Direct, an organisation with past experience of the establishment of such Trusts at other clubs.

Personal Recollections – Colin Slater.
A New Century – and a New Threat

Derek Pavis, a former Nottingham Forest vice-chairman, succeeded Jack Dunnett as chairman and majority shareholder of Notts on 2 June, 1987. In the early Nineties, with Neil Warnock as manager, Notts achieved two successive promotions, each via the play-off route, again to reach the pinnacle of the English game - the First Division.

As his 70th birthday approached Pavis gave his first intimation of his desire to sell his interest in Notts. The first serious negotiations took place with Reg Brearley, who had been chairman of Sheffield United in the Eighties and had attracted unfavourable publicity then and in subsequent football dealings in Scotland and at Grantham.

My stories so alarmed supporters that they led to the formation of SNAG - Support Notts Action Group - in August, 1999. Its officials met Mr Brearley at his home and said later: *"Nothing he told us gave us confidence that the club would be in safe hands."* Their avowed intention was to stop Brearley buying Notts and Pavis told a shareholders' meeting later in the same year that there would be no deal.

SNAG basically comprised the same fans who, in December 2002, decided to form the Notts Supporters' Trust. They met for the first time in January, 2003 in the back room of Martin Naylor's house, little dreaming of the role they were to play in saving the club from folding. The Trust's initial leading figures were John Thornhill, who had been chairman of SNAG and was later replaced as Trust chairman by David Hindley, and Steve Thompson, a local solicitor who was to become the Trust's representative on the board of directors. But much was to happen before then.

After the end of the discussions with Brearley, Pavis continued to look for a buyer.

Step forward an American not entirely unknown on the Nottingham football scene, Albert Scardino. His earlier connection was a failed interest in seeking to take over Nottingham Forest, followed immediately by contact with Pavis, though the talks at that stage soon stalled. Later negotiations were more productive and on 15 November 2000 a sale agreement was signed between DCP Holdings Ltd (DCP) a company wholly owned by Derek Pavis and his wife Vivien and Notts Holdings Ltd (NHL) a company wholly or largely owned by Scardino (AS). This provided for the agreed purchase price to be apportioned, as between share capital and loan capital, so that around £320,000 was to be paid for DCP's 93% interest in the equity (shares) and approximately £2,100,000 for the loan capital owed on demand to DCP by the club.

Scardino declined personally to guarantee payment for the purchase of the shares and repayment of the loan capital. It was agreed that ownership of the shares would only transfer (from Pavis to Scardino) as each instalment of the price for the shares and loan was handed over. The first instalment of £106,667 for 31% of the shares and £565,633 in repayment of part of the loan capital were paid on the signing of the contract. Then came the first real sticking point. Scardino failed to pay the second instalments for the shares (a further £106,667) and loan (£832,183), due on 15 November 2001.

At the beginning of February 2002, Pavis publicly put pressure on Scardino by stating that he may try to regain complete control if the deal was not soon completed. Pavis explains: *"I waited for four months while Mr Scardino continued to try to raise finance. He told me that he was negotiating the provision of monies and facilities either by Nottingham City Council acting alone or in concert with GMAC. These monies did not materialise."* From his point of view Scardino saw it differently.

In a letter at the time he wrote: *"We have fallen off the schedule by three months or so, for a large number of reasons...As for the money not being there, we are about ten weeks late but we are on track for completion soon."*

On 5 March 2002 the parties sat down to thrash out and sign a new, restructured deal the terms of which were more favourable to Scardino. Once again the payments were to be made in three instalments, on 5 March and 31 May 2002 and on 5 March 2003. On the first date, when the revised deal was signed, the first repayment was made. The following day Scardino wrote to staff: *"It should come as a relief to us all that we have now found a way forward. We have a lot of things to do to bring things right."* But when the second instalment was due (on 31 May) Scardino defaulted again.

In effect, he signed two agreements to buy the club – the first on 15 November, 2000, the second on 5 March, 2002. In each case he made the initial "deposit" as agreed. But he subsequently did not pay the balance of the "mortgage" as also agreed. The result was swift and savage.

On 17 June 2002, Notts County was put into administration with debts of £6m.

Scardino describes himself as a "trailing spouse", coming to England when his wife Marjorie's business brought her here from the States. For 25 years he had been what he describes as "a hack" - a reporter, editor, small-newspaper operator and then a government press officer. His philosophy was: *"Find a club that had an adequate stadium, a metropolitan area of some size and manageable debt - and it might be possible to have much the same effect on a community's psyche as if you had a local paper. We eventually found Notts County. As the 2001-02 season approached the board decided to take a gamble by spending more in the transfer market than we had planned. But things went awry."*

The question of Notts debts at the time of the takeover produced such a spat between Pavis and Scardino that in October, 2002 a statement had to be carried in the club's official programme: *"Comments in the Press attributed to Albert may have implied that Derek Pavis was to blame for financial mismanagement which brought the club to its present state. The board would like to make it clear that at the time of the takeover on 15 November 2000 the club was cash positive and solvent and no such blame or criticism was intended."*

So just what caused Notts to be in such a financial state? What Scardino described *as "a gamble"* in signing six new players *at inflated salaries* in the summer of 2001 contributed as much as anything. The players brought in were Steve Mildenhall and Stuart Garden (goalkeepers), Ian Baraclough and Darren Caskey (midfield), Marcel Cas (winger) and Tony Hackworth (striker). Those behind the recruiting of them were manager Jocky Scott and deputy executive chairman Peter Storrie, appointed with responsibility for much of the day-to-day running of the club with an office at Meadow Lane, while Scardino commuted from his London base. The pair were introduced when Storrie was chief executive of West Ham United.

Three of the new players - Caskey, Baraclough and Hackworth - were paid salaries of more than £100,000 per annum, as were two existing players. Cas was not far below that figure. The "gamble" would pay off *only* if Notts were promoted to the First Division. The season started poorly and as early as October, 2001 manager Scott and the club parted company, Gary Brazil being called up for the second time from the assistant's role to take over. Not that this lasted for long, either.

On 5 January, 2002 - third round FA Cup day - Notts didn't have a game. Mansfield Town lost at Leicester City, after which their manager Billy Dearden told the players he was leaving for a club in a higher division.

The same evening Storrie celebrated his 50th birthday with a dinner party at Ashmore's Restaurant, Radcliffe-on-Trent. I was pleased to be among the invited guests and was already there when the new Notts manager arrived: Dearden, with his wife, Judith. They were seated at the same table as Brazil – and me. *"Only with Dearden's appointment did we begin to get a grip,"* says Scardino.

Dearden was believed to have accepted the post on the undertaking that he would have a limited amount of money to spend on transfers. In less than a month he and fans were stunned when the Football League slapped a transfer embargo on Notts, who had been forced to borrow money from the Professional Footballers' Association to pay players' wages after the postponement of two home games in January. As if Dearden's arrival and a transfer embargo were not enough, January 2002 produced another unexpected shock. Storrie agreed to work for Portsmouth FC for two days a week.

Scardino sought to soothe supporters' anxieties in a letter: *"Peter's gig at Portsmouth is a win-win for the club. They get him for two days a week, they pay for three (money for Notts, not Peter) for five weeks, at a time when we are strapped for cash. He gets to spend time with his buddy Harry [Redknapp] in the hopes of enlisting his help to find a home for several of our overpaid and underperforming players."* Scardino followed this up with another letter 24 hours later: "Portsmouth would very much like to hire Peter as chief executive. They've done a good job of leaking that in the hopes that they will persuade him to jump. But he has a contract with Notts County, a considerable personal investment in the club and a real affection for the community." Suffice further comment on Storrie's situation except to add that he *did* become chief executive at Portsmouth.

The game at Swindon was Dearden's third in charge. He had been given a huge welcome by the travelling Notts fans when he stepped out at Cambridge to take charge of his first match, which Notts won 2-0. It turned out to be a false dawn. Notts lost eight of their next ten matches and drew the other two. They did not secure their second win under Dearden until the beginning of March. With the club in 23rd position in the League and with only ten matches to go, relegation was fast becoming a real probability.

Notts then proceeded to win four matches in a row, without conceding a single goal and were to lose only twice more before the last match of the campaign – at Meadow Lane against Huddersfield Town. What drama! Notts simply *had* to win to avoid relegation. Some 15,600 spectators turned up to see a 2-1 home victory. Finishing 19th Notts were safe, an outcome greeted with scenes of delirium as fans swarmed on to the pitch demanding the presence of the players on the balcony in the main stand, in front of the boardroom. A bemused Dearden said to me in a post-match interview, carried live on BBC Radio Nottingham: *"These fans are just amazing."*

They proved how amazing when Scardino launched *"The Great Escape Fund"* to enable the Football League's transfer embargo to be lifted. The response so exceeded needs that it was announced in mid-March that the surplus would be used as a feeder for a player purchase fund. Scardino described the response as astonishing, adding: *"Dozens of supporters came forward to make donations. The amounts we received varied from £20 to more than one contribution of £25,000, far exceeding anything we had expected. We are both grateful and proud of those who support this team. We are still a long way off solving all the financial problems, but with this level of support we will get there sooner rather than later."*

Enter the Administrator

Precisely three months after this euphoric statement, and three months after the end of the season, Notts went into administration. Paul Finnity (who was to have the highest profile) John Kelly and Gurpal Johal, partners at Kroll Buchler Phillips, were duly appointed by the High Court as Joint Administrators on 17 June, 2002. The Administration Order was made chiefly to secure Notts' survival and to put in place a Creditors' Voluntary Agreement (CVO).

Kroll stated that the primary cause of the club's financial crisis was the inability to convert short-term debts to long-term mortgage, plus insufficient revenue over recent years which had resulted in mounting debts. The ongoing takeover negotiations had, to a lesser extent, contributed to the current plight. They assured fans that they had no immediate plans for any sale of players or for staff redundancies. Kroll also said: *"Despite discussions with both Nottingham City and County Councils, it has not been possible to achieve a solution to the club's financial problems."*

Scardino, speaking as the club's acting chairman, was furious at what he perceived as lack of public support from the two major local authorities. The City Council said they were unwilling to act as guarantors for a life-saving bank loan and a bigger crisis was only averted when four of the six directors agreed to inject £120,000 to help to keep the club going during the summer. Scardino snapped: *"The City Council reneged on a six-month commitment to participate in a financial assistance plan, placing the club's future in doubt. Everything is at risk because the City Council decided not to keep its promise."* On their assurance that they would be able to complete their fixtures, Notts were allowed by the Football League to start the new 2002-03 season. Scardino remained bullish, suggesting that Notts would still be playing football years ahead.

After a shaky period - Notts were in the relegation zone at the end of November and only just outside it in mid-January - they finished in a relatively healthy position, 15th in the Second Division. Mark Stallard's 24 League goals made a massive contribution to reaching safety, especially during a late run when Notts lost only twice in eleven matches. But greater dramas were taking place off the field.

Nottingham City Council clarified its position in a letter dated January, 2003, with the significant statement that they had approved the terms for the surrender and grant of a new 250-year lease to the club (of the Meadow Lane ground) *"subject to satisfactory assurances being given that the restructuring of the lease will secure the future of the club. The draft lease has now been produced and forwarded to the solicitors acting for the administrator."*

The letter also lifted the lid on some of the background to what had been going on. *"The club was originally going to raise funding through a development company called Roch...I understand that Roch will not be able to consider continuing with the investment until nearer the summer. This is clearly not acceptable; the administrator is considering other options."* It also stated that a leading Labour member of the City Council, John Taylor, had indicated interest from British Waterways Board/ISIS, who were involved in the waterside regeneration area, but that this offer was no longer available.

The City Council letter raised the spectre of *"the possibility of a ground share arrangement with Nottingham Forest"*, an idea which always raises the ire of Notts fans. Finnity was to say at a later date: *"Without the new lease offered by the City Council the club would probably have no future."*

March 2003 was a month of feverish activity. Over 400 fans attended a crisis meeting on 12 March and only two voted against a proposal to set up a Supporters' Trust, on which so much work had been going on behind the scenes and membership of which quickly rose to 1,300.

Director Doug Ward, a local motor dealer, headed a consortium which had a first takeover bid refused, only to come back with a second offer, which was also rejected.

Another director, David Rhodes, was frequently rumoured to be on the point of heading a buy-out but nothing positive ever developed.

As the season's end approached efforts to find new owners intensified and, shortly before the last game came a statement with (as events proved) the somewhat over-confident heading:

MAGPIES' DEAL ALMOST DONE.

It disclosed that the prospective new owners were Raj Bhatia (40) a businessman from Essex with substantial interests in aviation and property industries and Frank Strang (45), based in the North of Scotland, also with aviation interests in addition to extensive interests in sports and leisure tourism. The two met in the mid-1980's when they were serving officers in the RAF. Bhatia said: *"Our role will be to ensure the long-term viability of the club - and allow the fans to support it without worrying about whether it's going to exist or not."* Finnity said: *"We are close, and although certain matters remain to be tied up and certain conditions met, I am confident that the deal will be done."*

Finnity invited Bhatia and Strang to be his guests at Meadow Lane on the season's last day to watch Notts beat Cheltenham. I met them both in Finnity's Nottingham city centre office on the previous day – Friday 2 May. I was told that Strang needed to fly back to Scotland as his wife was giving birth to their baby. Bhatia, however, was at the game, before which I interviewed him briefly, live on radio, finding him so diffident that I assumed he was microphone-shy. On further reflection there was perhaps more to his apparent unease than met the eye, though he had the professional advice of an astute public relations man, Sam McEwan.

Within a week Scardino was back in the frame with a new offer, reported to be in excess of £3m, having secured the backing of Quintain Estates, who are partners in the redevelopment of Wembley Stadium. They would take ownership of the Meadow Lane stadium, which Notts would lease back from them for between £200,000 and £250,000 a year. There would be enough money to bring Notts out of administration. Finnity accepted the offer as financially suitable.

Both the Bhatia-Strang and Scardino bids appeared to have the approval of the City Council and a power battle was already in prospect when a third party, Vantis Sports Solutions, namely Ken Anderson and Lawrence Goodman, joined the contest.

A Fateful Day

Friday 30 May was one of the momentous days of all, with separate meetings of creditors and shareholders in the Oriental Suite at Meadow Lane. All creditors received a 40-page statement from the administrators, with some dire warnings.

If the proposal to clear outstanding debts, leaving the way clear for the sale of the club, was not accepted by the creditors, **Notts County would cease to exist as a Football League entity.** The creditors seemed to be trapped between a rock and a hard place, because it was, rightly, anticipated there would be no money for unsecured creditors as a result of the sale of the business and assets. The *only* bodies which would receive *anything* were the Inland Revenue and Customs & Excise. The Revenue, owed £386,000, would get £42,350 (actually increased to £78,151 at the time of the settlement), Customs & Excise, owed £108,000, would get £11,770 (increased to £21,848).

Those who would receive nothing included past and present directors, supporters who had loaned money or taken out season-ticket bonds, and suppliers of various goods and services. Football-related debts at £327,000 would be treated separately and would become the responsibility of the new owners. Many people were to lose money, the heaviest losers being Scardino and Pavis, in that order, both of whom finished well over £1m out of pocket.

The creditors and shareholders gave the necessary approvals – in the creditors' case to a Company Voluntary Agreement. Save for two Government agencies all the creditors knew there was nothing in it for them. Kroll stated that final offers for the business and assets had to be received by the close of business on 30 May 2003.

As expected three bids were tabled. There was to be an anxious wait before, in early June, Bhatia-Strang were named as the preferred bidders, putting Scardino and Vantis out of the race. It is not thought to have swayed the administrators' decision but the possibility of Scardino being chosen caused some supporters actively to oppose it. The Supporters' Trust, while determined to maintain a genuinely neutral stance and show a willingness to work with whichever bid was accepted, conceded there was considerable concern among members about Scardino's continuing involvement. A group of them, led by long-time supporter Sandra Lakin, launched a petition.

In the eyes of some supporters Scardino had never fully recovered from a controversial £145,000 sponsorship deal with a local estate agent under which the world-famous Meadow Lane was renamed the Aaron Scargill Stadium. The monies were to be received in nine instalments. Only the initial £5,000 was ever received before the estate agency's crippling financial problems were exposed.

Bhatia-Strang provided proof of finance to Kroll on 30 May 2003, but failed to complete the purchase before the meeting of the Football League board on Monday 4 August, as they had been required to do, to avoid the club being expelled from the League. Finnity said: *"On Friday 1 August, when they had not one penny available, I think Raj Bhatia and Frank Strang were in shock. Their bid failed at a very crucial moment where we only had from Friday to Monday, when we could potentially have been thrown out of the League."*

On that fateful Friday Notts played a pre-season friendly match against Royal Antwerp. It was abundantly clear to me that the Bhatia-Strang deal was unravelling - fast. Virtually the whole of the close season had been wasted on an abortive bid. Now the new season was only a week away.

On the Sunday morning my peace was suddenly shattered at 9.41 by a surprise telephone call from Finnity in which, for the first time in my hearing, he used the word "crisis". Coming from him, a man not given to hyperbole, it indicated a new depth of seriousness. Finnity's invitation was to go to his office in Park Row, Nottingham, later that morning for a full briefing. We met at 11.30 for 90-minutes when he confirmed how bleak the situation was.

He asked me to return in the early part of the evening. When I did so he was with two other men. One was Peter Joyce, a director of Notts, and Roy Parker, a former director of Leicester City who I had met several months previously when he had first shown interest in investing in Notts, though talks with Pavis soon proved abortive. Now he seemed to be prepared again to get on board, no doubt at the instigation of Joyce.

As the person largely responsible for Joyce joining the board in the first place I sincerely believe great credit is overdue to him for his timely efforts to mount an eleventh-hour rescue attempt in the most dire of circumstances.

Finnity could not reach his firm's press and public relations advisers and asked me to assist him in preparing a statement. It said: *"The administrator will look for certainty as the preferred bidder has failed to complete the takeover despite repeated, categoric and emphatic assurances from the consortium and its advisors that they could deliver"* In a personal statement Finnity added: *"This is a devastating blow at this late stage, almost nine weeks after the preferred bidders were identified."*

The first casualty of the Bhatia-Strang collapse was Geoffrey Richmond. The former Bradford City chairman had been named in June as chief executive. To say that his appointment was a surprise would be an under-statement, one reason for that being that there were strong and persistent rumours linking Queen's Park Rangers' chief executive David Davies with the post. Richmond was given responsibility for running the club on a day-to-day basis, but did not have a seat on the board and was not investing any of his own money. His stay was to last only two months.

It also brought an end to Paul Garland's association with Notts. He had come in as 'football adviser' to Bhatia and Strang. I witnessed how close Garland got to players and Dearden never seemed totally at ease with him. Finnity meantime secured an extension to the Football League deadline to early September. It was to be the first of several extensions amid fears that the League's patience was running out.

There is no greater Notts loyalist than John Mounteney, who served as vice-chairman over many years, first to Jack Dunnett and then Derek Pavis. He joined forces with the Joyce-Parker duo, while making it clear he did not want a seat on the board in return for his investment. Joyce became the public face of the group which became known as the Blenheim Consortium, for which it was not all plain sailing. One month into their efforts to secure the club - in September, 2003 - their major backers withdrew. Bob Wilson, head of a Leicester-based company, actually met Football League representatives but said they were allowing insufficient time for all the necessary legal and financial processes to be completed.

Around the same time came a further surprise. Magnum Power plc, of London, put a new offer in writing to Kroll. *"Magnum Power remains very interested in bidding for the assets and undertakings of Notts County in conjunction with Raj Bhatia... We believe that the League and the Council are very comfortable with Raj and Magnum as the new owners/operators of the club. Magnum would be the ownership and financing vehicle for our bid if we were invited back into the process. Our revised offer is £500,000 at completion, £2,550,000 by 31 December 2003."*

To many, the Blenheim Consortium's efforts appeared the more credible and, through its secretary, Nigel King, the Supporters' Trust made a significant step towards their ultimate partnership. He asked for a meeting with the Blenheim Consortium. This was set up for 5 September at Kroll's Nottingham office between the Trust and Joyce, Parker and Mounteney. An eleven-hour session was described by one Trust member who was present as *"tense and at times unproductive."*

It was, though, marked by a sensational development. A long-time Notts supporter, who is also a local businessman, telephoned to say he was willing to be a substantial investor, included in which he was willing to buy the Meadow Lane stand, hitherto owned not by the club but by Pavis, as it had been by Dunnett before him. The City Council was stipulating that, whoever the new owners of the club were, they also had to purchase the stand, otherwise the new lease on the ground would not be granted. The new investor insisted at that stage, and for some time afterwards, on complete anonymity while the Trust embarked on raising £250,000 to help towards survival - and give it a seat on the reconstituted board.

The Trust negotiated with the City Council that they would underwrite any shortfall. A massive bucket collection was organised on the day of Luton Town's visit to Meadow Lane - 6 September, the day after the key meeting between the parties at Kroll and a day which, because of Football League deadlines, supporters - many of them in tears - thought would be the club's last ever. The League actually allowed a further, final extension to 9 December.

Peter Joyce said: *"Until today I didn't realise how much people cared. When you see grown men crying out of fear that we could go under you know you are doing the right thing."* As the Trust said afterwards: *"The response was incredible. We were overwhelmed with donations from people of all ages. Many fans from other clubs turned up to help. One girl emptied the copper from her moneybox into the bucket; we were all deeply moved. We thought we might collect £10,000 but the final figure was in the region of £50,000, a truly magnificent sum. We had never witnessed such an outpouring of affection for the old club."*

A fund-raising group of four spearheaded the Trust's efforts: Ken Carter, Richard Stanton, Martin Naylor and Stephen Thompson. They organised a charity match with "old boys" from Notts, with Steve Cherry in charge, and Forest, under Garry Birtles. More success as on the day - Sunday 5 October - there was a gate of over 10,000 and a profit of £34,000. There was now real public awareness and support for all the efforts to save Notts and a real expectation that Notts would come out of administration in November. It was not to be.

A meeting at the Lancashire offices of the Football League in October, involving the Blenheim Consortium and the Trust, produced shock waves. The League said that the £1.4m which was on the table was insufficient. The Trust said they felt betrayed. The solution was that the anonymous investor would buy the ground lease from the City Council and allow Notts to play at Meadow Lane for the duration of its term, 150 years. The Trust spokesman again: *"This was an incredible offer. It was the only option. Fans should appreciate that this really was it. Nothing else would save the club."* At a meeting a month later, on 17 November, everybody was satisfied that the deal would be done.

The Trust held one more major event, a dinner-auction held at the Royal Hotel, Nottingham, because its capacity of 350 was greater than anything Notts could offer. The evening of 6 December turned out to be a special one. Ex-Notts player, then Forest manager, Paul Hart was guest speaker. Ex-players Craig Short, Tommy Johnson, Dean Thomas, Tony Hateley, Les Bradd, Dean Yates and others were there. So too was the current longest-serving player, Ian Richardson, and his wife Debbie, who had gallantly raised money with her own bucket collection, standing outside the Asda store in West Bridgford.

Organiser Steve Thompson, who asked me to be MC, says: *"At the start of the evening our bank balance showed £212,000. I knew the City and County Council leaders, Jon Collins and Mick Warner, each wanted to make donations of £15,000. The silent auction and raffle raised £4,000. The auction produced £14,090. I could not believe it. We had reached £250,000. I was overwhelmed. The whole place went wild."*

After 18 months in administration the long-awaited climax was now approaching - **It came on Wednesday 3 December 2003.**

Finnity announced: *"The Football League has agreed to transfer Notts County's share in the Football League to the Blenheim Consortium, following the successful completion of the deal late last night. Key to securing the deal has been the ability to secure a new lease on the stadium."*

Kroll clarified the terms: *"The business and assets of the club were sold to the Blenheim Consortium for £2.7m. In addition the consortium acquired from DCP Holdings Ltd that company's interest in part of the stadium (The Meadow Lane stand). Should the club be promoted to the First Division (the Championship) prior to the 2006-07 season a further £250,000 will be payable."*

The Blenheim Consortium said the new board would comprise Joyce, Parker and Andrew Rigby (the nominee of the major investor) and

David Hindley (chairman of the Supporters' Trust, who shortly afterwards was replaced by Stephen Thompson). In a policy statement they immediately made it clear that the club would be run on more prudent lines: *"We will not allow expenditure to exceed revenue and we will be relying on home-grown product in all areas of operation. There are no short-term solutions."* The statement also promised a further statement *"before Christmas"* on the appointment of *"an established chief executive"* and said they hoped that a high profile individual would accept the offer of the chairmanship which they had made to him. No such statement ever followed and neither such appointment has ever been made, giving some to have real anxieties about the soundness of the structure of the club. There are two reasons why I share these doubts. Within five months of the takeover, though remaining a director (at least for the time being) Peter Joyce, sadly, chose to leave the scene, taking no active role in the club's affairs. And no chief executive was appointed.

Mills and Green on the Scene

The new owners gave no immediate hint of the managerial changes which followed only a month later with the departure of Billy Dearden and the arrival of a younger man, former Notts and Forest player Gary Mills from Coventry City, who had continued to live in Nottingham, to take charge. Dearden left on 7 January, Mills arrived two days later - all very streamlined on the part of those now in charge. Like Dearden over the previous two seasons Mills's immediate and greatest challenge was to stop the club from going down, which would be a miserable anti-climax after it had been saved from going under Unfortunately, results did not go his and Notts' way. Relegation, staved off in the last two years, was finally assured on 24 April when Notts lost at home to Port Vale.

It was only during the close season of 2004 that Haydn Green chose to make his role as well as his identity public.

It was still a closely-guarded secret when Central Television East Midlands studios, based in Nottingham, decided to make a 30-minute documentary on what they called The Battle to Save Notts County. Aware that I knew the mystery man's identity, producer Allister Craddock – an old BBC colleague and friend - asked me to say something about him, which I did in the following terms. *"He is doing this because he has a passion for Notts County. He could not bear the thought of Notts County going under. He has no ulterior motive, nothing but the survival of Notts County and goodwill towards them. They are remarkable motivations in a game of football packed with egos in which he does not appear to have an ego at all. That picks him out as a fairly remarkable individual in this game."*

Haydn Green has subsequently spoken and has revealed himself to having been a supporter since March, 1957. Having decided to contact the administrators and offer assistance, when he learned that the club's collapse was imminent, he ultimately decided to buy the lease on the ground. Why? *"The lease cost the club nothing but they were able to sell it to me, thereby raising funds to pay off debts and emerge from administration. I saw it as a means of enabling the club to start again with very low overheads. To my mind it made no sense whatsoever for the club to be burdened with a heavy rental.*

.

"The lease which I now have with the City Council is for 150 years. The rent they charge is dependent on the division we are playing in and is also adjusted for inflation. In turn I have granted the club an 'under lease', also for 150 years. The rent I receive is exactly the same as I pay the Council, except that if we reach the Premiership I will receive a profit."

In League Two (where Notts operate in 2004-05) the head lease and the under-lease are both valued at £15,000. This will be increase to £20,000 in the event of promotion to League One.

Green points out that, by comparison, Leicester City are committed to an annual rental in excess of £2m for their ground and adds this. *"When the original lease arrangement was drafted for Raj Bhatia it contained a restriction on the club's security of tenure to only three years, during which time an annual rental of £160,000 was to be payable. The three-year clause was reluctantly agreed to by the Council who felt that, in the absence of any other takeover offer, they had to agree to Bhatia's conditions."* Then he adds: *"Somehow, I do not think many Notts supporters would have been celebrating Christmas 2006 if this lease had been signed."*

What of his role with Notts? *"While I am not a director and not involved in the day to day running of the club I am prepared to assist the board in seeking further opportunities in connection with the ground and its surroundings. We will seek to identify and exploit any and every opportunity to boost the club's finances."* Of the 18-month period in administration Green makes two observations.

He says a mistake was made over not checking out Raj Bhatia's resources. *"For six months he was given preferred bidder status. At no time was he asked to supply a set of accounts or bank statements to confirm his financial status. It has emerged that at the time of his supposed takeover he was in fact seeking a job as a pilot."* He also recalls attending the meeting with the Football League in October 2003 which so alarmed the Supporters' Trust. *"Our reception was demoralising. They made it clear they were not prepared to accept the administrator's plan. Instead of agreeing to the proposed initial payment of £1.4m they wanted the full £3.2m paid up front and said we should show we had sufficient resources to meet the club's estimated losses over the next 20 months, another £1m. The League had raised the bar from £1.4 to £4.2m without any warning. They made it clear we had two months to find the money or lose league status. They said they had run out of patience."*

Looking to the future Green says: "We are a debt-free club which has the resources to become self-financing. On the other side of the coin, there is no prospect of anyone putting further funds into the club aside from commitments already made. Nor will we mortgage the future and spend money we have not earned. *"We need a structure which limits the capacity of anyone to inflict damage. I would personally like to see both the Supporters' Trust and Supporters' Club play a bigger role in our future. The way football is run at present doesn't work effectively. We must be prepared to entertain radical change. Now is a good time for the dialogue to begin. I hope that supporters will wish to participate."*

Tony Cuthbert was company secretary before administration and carried on manfully during 18 traumatic months. He, too, has been reflecting, first on the initial 'highs' of the Scardino-Storrie era. *"They generated great excitement. There was great expectancy that big things were about to happen. Storrie went out of his way to build up the expectations of fans in his statements to the media. In hindsight, this only made matters worse. Our staff suffered even more than supporters. It was difficult to convince them that all would eventually be well."*

For my part, I remember how people said in 1965 that Notts wouldn't have been wound up; that if Bill Hopcroft had not come forward, some other benefactor would have appeared. What I know is that no other such person could be seen anywhere on the horizon. I suppose there may now be those who, reflecting on the events of 2002-03, may similarly say that if, Haydn Green had not stepped in, somebody else would have done so. I see absolutely no evidence for that.

No, on both occasions Notts were just, and only just, saved by the selfless generosity of two men. And it is not mere coincidence that they came not from some other country, or another part of our own country, but were Nottingham men through and through who cared deeply about the world's oldest League club, which happened to be in their midst and needed their help.

The audience at a Supporters Trust meeting at Meadow Lane on 3 April 2003.

Notts County crisis: EXCLUSIVE

- Latest rescue bid in tatters
- Tearful Pavis: Our darkest day
- Just five days left to save club

ON THE BRINK

1862

By PAUL TAYLOR

NOTTS County could go out of business if a new buyer for the club is not found within FIVE days.

The world's oldest Football League club was today plunged into fresh crisis, after the latest takeover deal collapsed.

The financial backers for the consortium, led by former Leicester City directors Roy Parker and Bob Wilson, have pulled out.

It leaves the Magpies needing to come up with a new deal by Monday — or face the prospect of being thrown out of the Football League.

Former chairman Derek Pavis broke down in tears as he labelled it "the darkest day in the history of the club", which stretches back more than 141 years. He said the club's hopes are now pinned on London businessman Raj Bhatia, who still hopes to put together a viable offer in conjunction with Magnum Power.

"We have to hope now that somebody sees what is happening and comes forward," said Mr Pavis. "This is a desperate, desperate time. I fear the worst because time is running out.

Full story: Back Page

Notts County's continued existence is on a knife-edge on 3 September 2003.

Anxious supporters gather outside the ground on 31 August 2003 to hear the latest news and fund-raising plans from David Hindley, the interim Chair of the Notts County Supporters Trust.

The collection buckets are out at what is feared could be Notts County's last-ever game, at home to Luton on 6 September 2003.

Mark Stallard has just scored Notts' second goal against Chelsea at Stamford Bridge in the Carling Cup on 29 October 2003. Notts lost 4-2 but both the team and their 3,000 travelling supporters won the respect of the Chelsea crowd. County's £300,000 share of the gate receipts provided a much-needed financial boost.

Paul Heffernam in action in the cup match at Chelsea.

Notts finally came out of Administration on 3 December 2003.

The programme cover for the Wycombe game on 13 December 2003 proclaims the success of the different groups whose combined efforts had saved the club. One supporter contributed £3 million but preferred to stay out of the limelight.

Magpies' £4.2m takeover deal sealed

NOTTS SAVED

By PAUL TAYLOR

THE future of Notts County has finally been secured.

The *Evening Post* understands that the £4.2m deal to take over the world's oldest Football League club was finished late last night, ending almost two years of crippling uncertainty for the Magpies.

The Blenheim consortium, which includes former directors Peter Joyce and John Mounteney, former Leicester City board member Roy Parker and the supporters' trust, are officially the new owners of the club.

And within the next few days, the Magpies should finally move out of administration after a [illegible]-day financial nightmare.

The deal was finally ratified when Football League officials gave their approval to the agreement and officially restored the Magpies' membership — or share — in the league.

The staff, players and management were informed first thing this morning.

WE'VE DONE IT: Peter Joyce (back, centre) celebrates with Notts County staff this morning

Yore Publications

(Established 1991 by Dave Twydell)

We specialise in football books (only), normally with an historic theme.
Including **Football League club histories**, over 30 to date.....
Reading, Bolton Wanderers, Partick Thistle, Rochdale, Torquay United, Scarborough, etc.
(We were the publishers of the highly succesful Official Notts County history
in 1995 - now out of print)

Also players **'Who's Who' books**, recent clubs include:
Queens Park Rangers, Oldham Athletic, Portsmouth, Hull City, Chesterfield......

Other titles of a more unusual nature include:
'The Ultimate Directory of English and Scottish Football League Grounds" (an impressive encyclopaedia detailing every ground on which a League match has been played)
'Through The Turnstiles Again' (A history of football related to attendances)
'Rejected F.C.' (A series of books providing the histories of former Football League clubs.
Plus non-League - The **'Gone But Not Forgotten'** series
(histories of defunct non-League clubs and former grounds)

Free newsletters (for details of these and many other titles) are issued biannually,
for your first copy please send a s.a.e. to:

Yore Publications, 12 The Furrows, Harefield, Middx. UB9 6AT

(website: www.yore.demon.co.uk)